WITHDRAWN

EVANGELISM
in a
Tangled
World

Wayne McDill

BROADMAN PRESS
Nashville, Tennessee

© Copyright 1976 ● Broadman Press.

All rights reserved.

ISBN: 0-8054-6214-7

4262-14

Unless otherwise indicated, all Scripture quotations are taken from *The New International Version*, copyright ©1973, The New York Bible Society International. Used by permission.

Scripture quotations marked NASB are taken from the *New American Standard Bible*, ©The Lockman Foundation, La Habra, California, 1971. Published by Creation House, Inc., Carol Stream, Illinois.

Scripture quotations marked KJV are taken from the King James Version.

Scripture quotations marked RSV are taken from the Revised Standard Version.

Dewey Decimal Classification: 269
Subject Headings: EVANGELISTIC WORK / / SALVATION

Library of Congress Catalog Card Number: 76-39712
Printed in the United States of America

Preface

This is Wayne McDill's first book, and it is an excellent reflection of its author. Wayne is one of the young evangelism strategists in a denomination that consistently baptizes over 400,000 converts each year. He represents a mature synthesis of a process of thinking about evangelism which has been taking place over the past 25 years. Both in classroom and denominational position and in the pulpit I have been witness to this thinking.

In the late 1940s and early 1950s *evangelism* was a magic word. There was a very naive and uncritical acceptance of everything that labeled itself evangelism. There was an almost total preoccupation with the gospel and a matching lack of interest in, and awareness of, the radical and rapid changes taking place in society. Everyone was so excited about the successes in suburbia that hardly anyone noticed that in small towns, open country, and the inner city the church was in trouble.

The 1960s were years of reaction. I was in the seminary classroom during this time and got the full impact of a generation of students in reaction. They were nervous about the church and looking for viable alternatives. They were fascinated with social work. They were intoxicated with Harvey Cox and *The Secular City*. They weren't too sure about being ministers. The majority tended to caricature evangelism as manipulative, shallow, and irrelevant to the needs of modern man.

The 1970s have seen a synthesis of these two eras. Wayne McDill is an excellent example. This generation cannot return to an uncritical acceptance of everyone's definition of evangelism. But it is unwilling to accept any approach to the Christian religion that ignores the uniqueness of the gospel of Jesus Christ and the way in which it speaks to the deepest and most profound needs of modern man.

While this generation now faces the celebration of "man come of age" as being somewhat premature, yet it sees the need of a better understanding of the context in which the gospel is shared and the church established.

Evangelism in a Tangled World is a most comprehensive book about evangelism for today. It deals honestly with the biblical roots. It deals with today's world with sensitivity. And it deals honestly and realistically with the call for evangelism strategies. The style of writing is so readable and the issues so central that it will be very helpful to every Christian who takes seriously sharing Jesus Christ.

Kenneth Chafin

Houston, Texas

Contents

1 Unraveling a Tangled World 7

2 Being Narrow and Liking It 25

3 Leave Us Happy Pagans Alone 43

4 Repainting Ancient Pictures 59

5 A Faith that Looks Before It Leaps 77

6 The Moving Parts of Conversion 93

7 The Gospel in Plain Clothes 111

8 Applying the Great Commission 129

9 Keys to Motivation 149

10 Disciplined to Win 165

1
Unraveling a Tangled World

I entered the restaurant that morning with the kind of comfortable feeling you have when you're dropping by to see your favorite aunt. Sitting down at a table, I took little notice that the chair was plastic. As the waitress took my order she placed a small cup of water before me—a plastic, throwaway cup. *That's odd,* I thought, as I began to look around a little more closely. This was different. It didn't have that quiet, comfortable, homey atmosphere I had expected.

One whole wall of the restaurant was a fancy new coffee bar for the waitresses with everything conveniently within reach— including the instant tea machine. As I fingered my plastic water cup I was beginning to get a little uneasy. Then the waitress brought my coffee. It had suds on top. *What kind of coffee is this?* I wondered. *Maybe there was still soap in the bottom of the cup.* Then I got my answer as I looked up toward the space-age coffee bar. There the waitresses were getting coffee from a spewing, sudsing, instant coffee machine. I groaned inside.

In so many very mundane ways we encounter almost daily the reality of a rapidly changing pattern of life. Much of it we really appreciate. Air conditioning, electric dishwashers, cordless electric hedge trimmers—what a convenience these things are. That old question "What will they think of next?" can hardly be answered fast enough these days. But in addition to the new gadgets given us by zealous manufacturers, other changes have to do with social patterns, morality, religion, and politics. Unless we are really "tuned in" to the latest news on these fronts, we can quickly get out of touch with our world.

When I was a child my mother had a wonderful talent for untying knots. No matter how tangled the piece of string I brought her, she would patiently work with it with nimble fingers until it was unraveled again, to my delight. Unraveling string is one thing. Untangling the ideas and trends of contemporary life is quite another. There seems to be one thing certain about modern life—its complexity.

In the current craze for nostalgia, as Americans look back to the thirties, forties, and fifties, there is surfacing again the desire for simpler times, less complex circumstances, more understandable values and trends. One of the most often mentioned qualities of those wonderful days of the past is simplicity. But since we cannot go back, maybe the only thing left for us is to try to understand our own day. Maybe we can identify some of the factors characterizing modern life that particularly affect evangelism. Perhaps we can break the confusion down into more workable portions which can be better understood.

How important is it for evangelism that we understand our day? Isn't the gospel an ageless message? Isn't the command to take that good news to every person still in force? If that is so, then why waste our time trying to unravel a tangled world? It is true that the ageless message of the gospel does not change no matter what the contemporary situation. The style and the language may change, but the basic truth that "God was in Christ, reconciling the world unto himself" (2 Cor. 5:19, KJV) does not change.

We must understand our tangled world to some degree at least if we are to effectively bring the good news of Christ to it. I do not promise here to explain every complexity of contemporary life. That kind of work must be left to the social scientists. What we will do is sketch the modern situation in rather broad strokes as it presents a challenge to evangelism. Then we will offer a biblical response to place the modern scene in the right perspective.

What Ever Became of the Good Old Days?

There is plenty of bad news in modern life. The world seems to be hurtling beyond our control in directions that cause us discouragement and fear. Our natural resources are running out. Pollution is spoiling our air, our water, our landscape. Every year millions more fall under oppressive dictatorships around the world. Economic troubles send businesses, cities, and even nations down to ruin. All of the bad news out there is further complicated by the bad news within ourselves. Modern man suffers from the inner anxieties, the frustration, the insecurity, the loneliness, the seeming restlessness of our day. All of this is a part of our tangled world.

In his book *Future Shock* Alvin Toffler writes that there is one ultimate difference in today's world. The distinction which separates contemporary man from all other ages of men is "a stream of change so accelerated that it influences our sense of time, revolutionizes the tempo of daily life, and affects the way we 'feel' about the world around us" (1). Toffler writes that this speedup of change in every area of modern life has caused us to think of everything as temporary. All our thoughts have been colored by this impermanence. Our relationship with people, values, things, and our whole world is affected.

The future is rushing in on us so fast that it takes our breath away. Toffler says that we are suffering from "future shock." Things change so fast that people begin to feel like they're in a strange country. They suffer from confusion and homesickness for the "good old days." They may become so disoriented that they lose touch with reality and begin to withdraw into a make-believe world of their own.

The many changes characteristic of this age plus the tendency to see man himself as the center of everything have caused people to be more and more concerned about understanding themselves. Psychologist Seward Hilner says that "self-understanding may have once been a luxury for a few philosophers and saints but it is now a necessity for psychological survival" (2). When times were simpler and society was uncomplicated, people tended to take themselves for granted. In those days, they did not appear to suffer psychological damage from doing so. But now the turmoil and ferment of the world around us is reflected in our own outlook on life.

Writers in recent years have often come to the conclusion that man is "come of age." They believe that he is now able to take over a considerable measure of responsibility for both himself and for his world. Harold E. Hatt, in his book *Cybernetics and the Image of Man*, writes that this characteristic is the most distinctive feature about modern man. He says that today's man has "more self-consciously and more forcefully insisted on his own autonomy and self-dependence than any other generation of man" (3). It is because of man's attitude today that he is reluctant to see himself as someone who is responsible to God.

Our contemporary environment has complicated the challenge evangelism faces in the modern world. The different world we live in has caused us to think differently. The constant pressure of the general outlook of today's world has a "programming" effect on us as it confronts us at every turn. Marshall McLuhan says that the entire pattern of thinking for modern man has changed, that he has been "massaged" by modern communications media which have brought the world in upon him like a "global village" (4).

The very fact of our shrinking world raises questions for evangelism never faced before. It is now possible to have almost instant satellite communication worldwide. We have watched on live color television men standing on the moon. Roger Shinn has pointed out that when George Washington was elected to the presidency in 1789 a messenger on horseback took seven days to bring him the news. Now the television networks use electronic computers to tell us the results of elections before the polls close (5). Even now supersonic transport planes like the British-French Concorde can speed passengers from Paris or London to New York in less than four hours. What does this revolution in transportation and communication mean for evangelism? The challenge and the opportunity are overwhelming.

Other questions raised by the modern scientific and technological revolution call upon us to rethink the meaning of evangelism in a tangled world. Will the population explosion be curbed, or must we face the responsibility of bringing the gospel to twice as many souls in a few short years? What will studies in parapsychology tell us, if anything, about the spiritual and psychic dimensions of man? Will drugs that change moods and even change personality be used to dull guilt and cure the symptoms of man's fragmented nature so that regeneration seems unnecessary? Will new psychological studies increase our understanding of the factors involved in conversion—decision, conviction, understanding? Will life in an affluent society provide such comfort and security that men will laugh at the idea of heaven?

If It Feels Good, Do It

I have seen several bumper stickers recently with the motto "If it feels good, do it." This and other expressions of a freewheeling morality are shrugged off as part of the complexion of our day. In the not-too-distant past they would have been considered obscene by most Americans. But a new moral climate, led by the "sexual revolution," has permeated every facet of our society. The real character of the change is not that men are any more immoral than they used to be. The change seems to be in the direction of a more public immorality—a frank and open, often blatant, expression of disregard for traditional moral values.

Generally, the shift in ethics has been from an emphasis on accepted standards for morality toward an emphasis on the unique situations that call for ethical decisions (situation ethics). Some writers, even among Christians, say that we should never try to decide in advance what our choices will be in moral decisions. The situation itself should be the final determining factor in whatever we decide is right or wrong. Even if we have rules that we believe we should follow, we should be ready to throw them out if the situation seems to call for it. Rather than having guidelines and laws, this approach would put the burden for right decisions on each individual as he is able to decide in the situation he is facing at the moment. Carl F. H. Henry has written in this regard that "the soul of the twentieth century man no longer feeds on objective and eternal norms, but is content with ethical leftovers" (6).

There is uncertainty about acceptable behavior not only among ordinary people but among the scholars and writers who are supposed to know something about it. Rather than beginning with God and what he has to say about moral values, most writers of ethics today begin with man. They analyze his identity. They describe his needs. They go to great lengths to spell out his philosophical and emotional problems. The beginning point of any study of ethics will set the pattern for the conclusions that are reached. If we begin with man in our study of ethics, we come up with something that looks very much like man. On the other hand, if we begin with God in our desire to find out what is right and wrong, we come a great deal closer to a picture of godly behavior.

The trends in morality in our tangled world have produced the results we might have expected. Pornography has come to be an everyday fact of life. Magazine racks, movies, and television reflect standards of decency which even ten years ago would have been considered shocking. There are now approximately one half as many divorces taking place per year as marriages. Couples are not bothering to marry until they have sampled married life without making any marriage commitment. College and university rules have been thrown aside to avoid any conflict with the morals of the young people in the dorms. Scandals in government have disillusioned the American people to the point that their confidence in government officials is at an all-time low. Business ethics are reflecting the same low standards; corporation heads approve whatever means are necessary to make a profit or get a contract.

All of this is not to say that the whole nation has "gone down the tube" morally. There seems to be arising a moral reaction toward a return to decency and honesty. As never before, the people are looking for leaders who are honest and sincere. They have come to the conclusion that the problems are so complex that no one person, nor all of us together, can seem to come up with all the answers; it is better to have a person in leadership who is honest and decent than one who professes to have all the solutions. We can hope the trend toward moral laxity has reached a point of turning around so that the future will lead in the other direction. But these changes of trends are difficult to see until many years after the turn has come.

Religion: Made in Asia

One challenging characteristic of modern society is the pluralism. "Pluralism" means we have a rather large assortment of different kinds of people with different ideas. The aspect of pluralism most challenging to evangelism may well be the religious pluralism. A nationwide survey of university students indicates that attitudes toward religion are influenced as never before by Eastern thought. It is not only those involved in Eastern cults whose thinking has changed. An increasing number outside these groups has adopted a mystical outlook.

Thirty-four percent of the students surveyed said they believed that "God is in everyone" and that "we're all a part of God." In this view the Creator and the creation are all the same. Twenty-four percent indicated they were skeptical about belief in God or that they didn't believe in God at all. Another 33 percent of the students identified with the view that "God is a distinct supernatural being, separate from man." So the three groups—the mystics, the skeptics, and the theists—were all well represented in our pluralistic culture.

It is also most interesting to note from the survey an increasing interest in religion of some kind. The students were asked about which groups or disciplines they had participated in or were strongly interested in. Nineteen percent, almost one fifth, named one of the Eastern groups—Transcendental Meditation, Yoga, Zen, Divine Light Mission, Hare Krishna, and so forth. Another 20 percent named some form of the occult, psychic phenomena, and such. Forty percent named Christian fellowships or churches and 9 percent Judaism. In bringing the good news of Christ to a tangled world, we certainly face a challenge from religion in all forms.

A part of the influence of Eastern religions is seen in the attitude of the students toward truth. Only 37 percent indicated that they believed there are absolute truths. Of course the belief in ultimate and dependable truth from God is fundamental to a biblical faith. The majority of those surveyed, 51 percent said, "Truth is basically relative; what is right or true for you may not be right or true for me" (7). If the university student of today indicates what the general population will think tomorrow, we will surely face this outlook as we try to share the gospel with modern man.

Even beyond the college campus the religious scene reveals the complexity of our tangled world. Transcendental Meditation, originally a jet-set and counter-culture fad, has a following now among educators, politicians, and sociologists. The Black Muslims are involved in an aggressive enlistment campaign and are now admitting whites to their membership. The Jehovah's Witnesses and Mormons are among the fastest-growing groups in America. While all this is going on most of the main-line Christian denominations are merging, consolidating, cutting back on missions, and generally continuing to lose ground.

In spite of these discouraging trends, there is a growing hope in many quarters for a revival of biblical Christianity. Evangelical results are continuing to increase among evangelical churches and parachurch groups. Missions organizations have reported real revival in recent years in Indonesia, Korea, and other parts of Asia. Reports from within Communist China and the Soviet Union indicate increasing interest in the gospel and bring urgent calls for more Bibles and literature. In this country massive evangelistic campaigns are being launched year after year to get the good news to a tangled world.

Listening for the Whispering Philosophers

When I was in the fourth grade, I broke into serious drama for the first time. I played the part of a woodchuck who raised the rather philosophical question, "How much wood could a woodchuck chuck if a woodchuck could chuck wood?" I well remember boldly stepping forward to say my memorable line. I also remember that Mrs. Lentsch was just out of sight offstage to whisper my lines if I forgot. All of us felt a great sense of security in knowing that we could not fail to say the right thing. If we hesitated, Mrs. Lentsch's loud whisper would get us started again.

I have wondered whether modern man isn't in a similar situation today. He thinks he is expressing his own original, well-thought-out ideas. But in reality he is getting his cues from the whispering philosophers just out of sight offstage. Philosophical ideas seep into the corporate pool of thought like a fog floating in from the bay. The man in the street hardly knows he's being indoctrinated in the strangely blended climate of contemporary thought. From every side comes the steady pressure of philosophical ideas—television, radio, newspapers, government, social and political experts, chance conversations, and so forth. But how many people realize that these ideas come from the whispering philosophers offstage?

Let's sketch some of the philosophical ideas that are influencing contemporary thought. We may not be familiar with the philosophers who write the thick books promoting these positions, but we will recognize the basic ideas. If we are to understand our day, we will need to realize that behind the new ways modern man is thinking are a few basic philosophical ideas. There is really nothing mysterious about it. Though all of us have our philosophical moments, the man in the street does not fancy himself a philosopher. Yet when you confront him with the gospel of Christ he may respond with a canned comment that stems from one of these philosophies. That doesn't mean he believes in all the teachings of that position.

It simply means that he thinks he believes what he just said. At least it sounded pretty good.

One generally accepted idea is naturalism. Naturalism did not come out of man's inner conviction about himself but out of a scientific approach to life that analyzes all things on the basis of the scientific method. Only what can be studied with the five senses is to be considered real; there can be no supernatural. This idea has made its way into the thought of modern men until they have begun to think this way without knowing why. When applied to the Bible, naturalism insists that there can be no miracles or anything supernatural. Truth cannot be known by revelation from God. It must be discovered and verified scientifically. Therefore the biblical record must be cleared of all references to the supernatural and treated not as the revelation of God, but as interesting folk literature.

The trend at present, though, is toward a revival of supernaturalism. People have tired of the old attitude that only that which can be touched, smelled, tasted, heard, or seen can be counted as real. They are beginning to seek an understanding of that which is beyond the five senses. Studies in parapsychology have moved contemporary thinking in this direction. Men are beginning to wonder about the unseen realm of the psychospiritual. The biggest audience for those late-evening talk shows are tuned in when the guest is a psychic or a witch, has seen creatures from other planets, can tell the future from measurements in the Great Pyramid, or has done experiments in ESP.

Another idea current today is secularism. This idea also came from outside of man's understanding of himself. It came in part from the trend toward religious freedom being granted by government to all religious groups. This of course required the neutrality of government in matters of religion and led to a secularism which divorced life from religion. Man seems to be getting along very well without God, solving all his own problems, dealing with the basic issues of life in ways that are very acceptable to much of modern society. This attitude is seen as modern man thinks of religion as a "take it or leave it" option. "You get your kicks going to church," he might say. "I get mine playing golf. You don't try to convert me to religion, and I won't try to convert you to golf."

Another idea that has made its way into modern thinking is

humanism. Humanism is the belief that the whole universe revolves around man. He is seen as the final supreme being. There is really no need for God because man himself is the most important creature there is. Modern man has therefore come to think that religion is optional. Since Christianity declares that there is something basically wrong with man, it is incompatible with humanism. Humanism sees man as ultimately having vast potential for conquering his world, for succeeding in whatever he attempts, for doing the impossible if given enough time. Who needs God anyway? Why should anyone accept the crutch of religion? It's really only for old women and children.

We must not assume that modern people are all humanists or naturalists or secularists. It is true, though, that the many ideas that have been generally accepted as true come from these basic philosophical positions. Most people do not realize that their own viewpoint is connected to any particular philosopy. Two noted psychologists wrote that "modern man is so mesmerized by the prevailing scientific world view, he can hardly get out of it or beyond it sufficiently to be properly critical of it" (8). The same difficulty is faced as we try to be objective about any of the philosophies which have become such an integral part of our thinking.

Somebody will say, "Well, I don't know what good it is if you can't eat it or touch it or taste it or smell it. " This is an expression of naturalism. Someone else will say, "I just can't believe that man won't finally solve all of the great problems we are facing." This may be an expression of humanism which places supreme confidence in the capabilities of man. Someone else will say, "I just think we'd better keep religion out of politics, and it will work better that way." This is probably an expression of secularism even though the person who expresses it would not catalog it that way.

There are other philosophical ideas floating around in modern man's thinking. One of these could be called nihilism. This philosophy says that there is no objective way to prove whether anything is true. This leads to the belief in ethics that there is no such thing as good or bad. Morality is all relative. One person's idea of right is as good as another's. Nihilism is behind much of the revolutionary thinking of our day, which believes in tearing down everything that is. It sees everything as so bad that nothing can be done to improve it except to destory it.

Another idea is called existentialism. This philosophy places a strong emphasis on man's own experience and the decisions he makes. An individual is free and responsible for making himself what he is. Existentialism is a form of humanism that focuses inward on the life of the individual. We see its influence in the emphasis in religion today on experience. The important thing is not doctrine or tradition or morality. The important thing in existential religion is how you feel and what you experience. Maybe you've heard a statement like this: "I don't care anything about doctrine. I know my experience is real. That's what really counts."

And Now, a Word from Our Creator

Reviewing the complexities of a tangled world might lead to what some have called the "paralysis of analysis." We become numb with a sense of helplessness at getting a grip on our world. Where are the handles? In a world as complex as ours we in the work of evangelism often feel like one who would try to plow the sea. Wherever we go the surging tide seems to wash in on the furrow behind us. Wouldn't it be better, we ask, if we didn't know anything about our world so that we could charge out to win modern man to Christ in the blissful innocence of our ignorance? Why can't we just go back to presenting the plain old gospel to plain old people and hoping that they will get saved?

Our purpose in analyzing the character of a tangled world is not to make the work of evangelism more difficult or complicated. Our world is there. That's a fact. And it's there as it actually is. Our wish for simpler times will not simplify our day. Neither will our ignorance of its complexities make them go away. We seek to understand our tangled world because we are commanded to saturate it with the gospel. The character of our age does not change the content of the message. It only calls for a special sensitivity in proclaiming it.

But where is God in all of this? Why doesn't he say something? Has he changed his mind about his plans? Is God at work in a tangled world? If so, where? How do we get in on it? If we keep our eyes on the world long enough, we will certainly lose sight of the fact that God is still alive. He does still have plans. The world hasn't sneaked up on his blind side and caught him by surprise. It hasn't gotten out of control. He can still handle it. God has not changed; and neither has his purpose changed.

The Bible says that God is sovereign. This means that he is supreme, that he is king, that he is indeed God. As the sovereign heavenly Father, God answers to no one, asks nobody his advice, isn't required to explain his actions, and accomplishes in heaven and earth what is pleasing to him. The Bible, in the mighty poetry of faith, declares that his "is the greatness, and the power, and the glory, and the victory, and the majesty . . . exalted as head above all" (1 Chron. 29:11). Paul writes that he is "the blessed and only Ruler, the King of kings and Lord of lords, who alone is immortal" (1 Tim. 6:15).

The sovereignty of God is a key issue for those of us who would do the work of evangelism. Some have believed that since God is sovereign, he will save whom he will and damn whom he will; so there is no use in our bothering with evangelism. J. I. Packer points out, though, that just the opposite is true. The sovereignty of God in his grace is our only hope of success in evangelism. Packer says that apart from God's sovereign grace there is not even the possibility of evangelism's being fruitful. "Were it not for the sovereign grace of God, evangelism would be the most futile and useless enterprise that the world has ever seen, and there would be no more complete waste of time under the sun than to preach the Christian gospel" (9).

This is true because man, in the deadness of his human nature, is blind and deaf to the truth of the gospel. No amount of persuasion on our part can cause him to see it. At the same time, Satan continues to work at fostering, encouraging, and promoting man's unbelief and disobedience. How can we counter such a force as that? The sovereign power and grace of an Almighty God is our only hope. Otherwise we would be left to our own persuasion, our own eloquence, our own ability to bring about the conviction of sin and the revelation of the living Christ in the understanding of those we seek to win.

God is not only a sovereign God; he is also a God of holiness. Holiness is God's sacredness, his "otherness." The opposite of holiness might be commonness. God is ultimately and supremely uncommon. There is no one like him. The Christian, even in the modern world, cannot escape the challenge of God: "Be holy, because I am holy" (1 Pet. 1:15). We must approach the task of evangelism with a sense of our own distinctiveness in the world. We must refuse to accept the common solutions of the world. Ours is a solution for man's needs that is unique. We must maintain the distinctive uncommonness of the gospel message and guard against watering it down, adding to it, or compromising it with the world's answers.

Not only is God sovereign and holy, but he makes his nature and his will known to us in terms we can understand. This revelation of God was recorded in the Scriptures by men inspired by the Holy Spirit (2 Tim. 3:16). It was carefully guarded and preserved through the often hostile territory of man's own history. Today the Bible stands as the objective proof of God's desire to make himself known to us. He does not leave us to speculate concerning what might be pleasing to him, or how a man might know him and be acceptable to him. We can declare the good news of Christ with the certainty that faith comes by hearing the Word of God (Rom. 10:17). As we declare the truth of the written Word, the Holy Spirit will minister to the hearers of the truth of the eternal Word. We have God's promise that, even in a tangled world, his Word will not return to him void. It will accomplish what he intends for it; it will be effective in the purpose for which God sent it forth (Isa. 55:11).

God is also all-powerful. There is a basic, almost unspoken, conviction in the Scriptures that God is well able to accomplish what he has set out to do. He declares the reality of a victory already won (John 16:33), announces in advance the outcome of war with the enemy, Satan (1 John 4:4; Rev. 12:10-11), and urges his children on to worldwide exploits by his power (Matt. 28:18-19). As we approach the challenge of evangelism, we refuse to allow our own weakness to discourage us. Since God is all-powerful there is no obstacle so great, no problem so complex, no crisis so grave, no threat so fearsome that the heavenly Father cannot deal with it. We can go forth with the gospel of Christ without regard to whether our task is humanly possible (Phil. 4:13), socially popular (Matt. 10:28), or personally painful (2 Cor. 12:10). We know that he is "able to do immeasurably more than all we ask or imagine, according to his power that is at work within us" (Eph. 3:20).

The Bible also says that God is righteous. He is consistent with himself in every respect and refuses ever to act in a manner that is not in harmony with all that he is (Rom. 9:14). Because of this he has established laws that indicate what is acceptable and what is not acceptable to him. As we face the task of evangelism we can come to this responsibility, confident that there are absolutes of right and wrong which are rooted in the very nature of God. We are not at the mercy of uncertainty and speculation. We do not have to back away before the prevailing trends of relative morality. The Holy God has established his righteousness among men in terms of moral laws that they can understand. The weakness of human nature and the righteous demands of the law create a tension which opens the door for the good news of new life in Christ.

God is also immutable. This means that the nature of God, his purpose, and his Word do not change. God spoke through Malachi to say, " For I am the Lord, I change not" (Mal. 3:6). The New Testament also gives a clear statement of the unchanging character of God: "Like a garment they will be changed. But you remain the same, and your years will never end" (Heb. 1:12). James wrote graphically of the Father "who does not change like shifting shadows" (Jas. 1:17). If God is unchangeable, then we can be assured of his faithfulness to us. Not one word of all his promises has failed (1 Kings 8:56). We can approach the task of evangelism with a confidence in the permanence of the established order of God. We can see the corruptible and ever-changing fads of the world in their proper setting—against the backdrop of an unchanging God.

What's the World Coming To?

A vital factor for our approach to sharing Christ in a tangled world is the position of the world with respect to the purpose of God. The New Testament says that "the whole world is under the control of the evil one" (1 John 5:19), that the world is to a large degree under the sway of demonic powers. In fact, the terminology "the world" is used at times in Scripture to mean "the whole circle of earthly goods, endowments, riches, advantages, pleasures," which, "although hollow and frail and fleeting, stir desire, seduce from God, and are obstacles to the cause of Christ" (10). Paul writes of Satan as "the ruler of the kingdom of the air" (Eph. 2:2), the "god of this age" who "has blinded the minds of unbelievers, so that they cannot see the light of the gospel" (2 Cor. 4:4).

The contrast of that which is worldly with that which is godly touches the moral (1 Cor. 5:10), the intellectual (1 Cor. 3:19), the personal (1 Cor. 1:27), and the religious (Rom. 3:19). In our tangled world we must be sensitive to the contrast and aware of the continual struggle of the two opposing kingdoms. Schaeffer writes that "the Christian is to resist the spirit of the world. But when we say this we must understand that the world-spirit does not always take the same form. So the Christian must resist the spirit of the world in the form it takes in his own generation" (11). We recognize that very often we will face the gray areas where the ideologies overlap and the distinction is unclear. We know that we will need the maturity that comes in the practical application of God's truth and a growing moral and spiritual sensitivity (Heb. 5:14).

Though the world is corrupted, fallen, and alienated from God, that does not mean that there is no good at all in it. It is still true, as the psalmist wrote, that the "earth is the Lord's, and the fulness thereof; the world, and they that dwell therein" (Ps. 24:1, KJV). It is also true, as Paul believed, that God "works out everything in conformity with the purpose of his will" (Eph. 1:11). In the victory of the cross and resurrection, all cosmic powers were brought under the rule of Christ and became unwitting instruments in the redemptive purpose of God (Acts 4:25-28; 1 Cor. 2:8). God is at work in Christ to reconcile the world to himself (2 Cor. 5:19), and that purpose will be fulfilled until the kingdom of the world comes under the rule of God through the lordship of Christ (Rev. 11:15).

With this knowledge of the sovereign purpose of God, we see the world in its proper perspective. The earth is a planet in rebellion, dominated by a world system which stands in opposition to the authority of God. Nevertheless, it is still God's world. It is still full of the beauty of nature under the providence of God (Isa. 6:3). The truth of God is still operative in the natural order and in the human order. The very fact that society is in disorientation and spiritual confusion indicates that man has exchanged the truth of God for a lie (Rom. 1:25). So we do not set ourselves automatically against all that we find in the world. We rather discern in the midst of our environment those values, those philosophical viewpoints, and those moral positions which are worldly and those which are true to Scripture. Unless we operate on the basis of the stark contrast which the Scriptures set forth, we will find ourselves being influenced and weakened by the world system we are in God's purpose to transform.

So we face the challenge of bringing the good news to a tangled world with mixed emotions. There is no reason for a sense of perplexity and uncertainty as we examine the contemporary scene. Nonetheless, there is a better reason for hope and confidence as we then turn our eyes to the changeless and sure purpose of our God. The remainder of this book will be given, then, to presenting a biblical understanding of some of the key aspects of evangelism. Our purpose is to construct a biblical conception of the evangelistic task so that we may be reawakened to that distinctive outlook. We can hope, as we try to get a dependable perspective of our responsibility, that the challenge of sharing Christ in a tangled world will not be so threatening.

A knowledge of God's nature and sovereign purpose in Christ is our greatest source of assurance for the task of evangelism. Our conception of the nature and purpose of God is directly related in a dynamic fashion to our outlook on life, our strategies, and our methods for reaching the world for Christ. As we are confronted with the biblical concept of God we are forced to reinterpret all of reality from that viewpoint. But nothing is more effective in kindling a boldness and zeal for evangelism than a vision of our almighty God and his redemptive purpose. Daniel wrote that "the people who know their God shall stand firm and take action" (Dan. 11:32, RSV).

Notes

1. Alvin Toffler, *Future Shock* (New York: Random House, 1970), p. 16.
2. Seward Hiltner, *Self-Understanding Through Psychology and Religion* (New York: Charles Scribner's Sons, 1951), p. xi.
3. Harold E. Hatt, *Cybernetics and the Image of Man* (Nashville: Abingdon Press, 1968), p. 67.
4. Marshall McLuhan and Quenton Fiore, *The Medium Is the Massage* (New York: Random House, 1967), p. 63.
5. Roger Lincoln Shinn, *Tangled World* (New York: Charles Scribner's Sons, 1965), p. 15.
6. Carl F. H. Henry, *Christian Personal Ethics* (Grand Rapids: Wm. B. Eerdmans Pub. Co., 1957), p. 13.
7. Pat Means, "West Meets East: A Look at a Metaphysical Coup on the Campus," *Worldwide Challenge*, April 1976, 12-15.
8. Lowell Colston and Paul E. Johnson, *Personality in Christian Faith* (Nashville: Abingdon Press, 1972), p. 15.
9. J. I. Packer, *Evangelism and the Sovereignty of God* (Downers Grove, Illinois: Inter-Varsity Press, 1961), p. 106.
10. Thayer, *Greek-English Lexicon* (New York: Harper and Brothers, 1889), pp. 356-57.
11. Francis Schaeffer, *The God Who Is There* (Chicago: Inter-Varsity Press, 1968), p. 18.

2
Being Narrow and Liking It

He looked as though he were the discoverer of an original thought. He pursed his mouth and raised his eyebrows in a rather pious, all-knowing pose. "Well, Reverend," he crooned, "I just believe we are all trying to get to the same place. We may take different roads, but maybe we will all get there anyway." I can't count the times I've heard a statement something like that. It seems to be a part of American folk religion that we are all trying to get to the "same place," wherever that is. The other part of that viewpoint is that since there are so many different ways to get to that same place, we ought to look upon one another with kindness as we all take our different roads according to our own particular convictions.

Those who have been more narrow than that in their religious convictions have been frowned on as bigots or sectarians. I heard about a pastor of this type who was stopped on the street by a layman from another denomination. The layman said, "Excuse me, sir, but aren't you the pastor of that church that believes only their group is going to heaven?" The pastor didn't even pause at such a loaded question. "I'm probably the man you are thinking of," he replied. "But we don't believe only our group is going to make it to heaven. We don't even think all of our group will make it!"

In a pluralistic, liberal-thinking, broadminded day such as ours, it is not very popular to be narrow. Christians who believe that Jesus Christ is the only way to God and that a person must exercise an adult decision of faith in him are just not with the spirit of the day. Some of us who have been brought up in this narrow tradition have often chafed under these accusations. We have been forced to reexamine our position again and again. We have asked ourselves whether our narrow outlook should be modified to match the times.

Our critics have asked, "Why is it that some of you Christians think you have the only true religion? Why aren't you more broad-minded? After all, isn't there a lot of truth in all the religions of the world? Isn't it true that God is pleased with anybody who tries to worship in a sincere manner? Isn't it true that whatever approach people take to finding God is good even if it's not Christianity? Christianity may be one of the best ways to God, but does it have to be the only way?"

Beyond that we have heard questions like these: "Why don't all the religious people of the world get together? Couldn't those who worship God, whatever they think God to be, unite to form one great group? Then they could take a stand against all of the unbelieving atheists and pagans. They could make a united stand for religion and for God." There are a lot of people who think this sounds good, that this ought to be done, because they think there is nothing worse than somebody who does not believe in God at all.

Answering the Religious Question

What is the basic issue we are talking about? Can we reduce all these religious questions to one basic idea? Can we find that one human question all religions are trying to answer? Yes, I think we can. The religious question is this: "How can I be acceptable with God?" It may be that someone else would frame it in different words. Nevertheless, all these other questions finally boil down to this one religious question when it comes to the individual and his approach to religion—"How can I be acceptable with God?"

In every corner of the earth have been found people who are trying to worship one way or another. I heard about a tribe in the jungles of South America who had seen few, if any, outsiders. One day a plane flew over their jungle area, and from an open cargo hatch an advertising sign fell out. It was a sign advertising some kind of beer. These natives were amazed at the great silver eagle that flew over because they had seen very few planes. Theirs was a remote area, not on the way between anywhere and anywhere else. So in their fascination they set up a special worship center in their village and began to worship the beer sign. We may think they were ignorant, primitive, and foolish. But a lot of civilized areas in the world have an idolatry not much different from theirs.

I have found that most people already know a lot about the religious question "How can I be acceptable with God?" Most people are aware of trying to find an answer for it. Why is this? I believe it is because the Spirit of God is making people aware of some very basic truths throughout the world. When you talk to someone about God he already knows several things because the Holy Spirit, in rather ordinary and yet sometimes mysterious ways, has convinced him of these facts. The Bible says that the Spirit "will convict the world of sin, and righteousness, and judgment" (John 16:8, NASB).

One day as I was studying in the city library, I fell into conversation with a young man who claimed to be an agnostic. He was an intellectual sort and seemed to be knowledgeable about the various forms of religion on campus at the university. As our conversation went along I asked him to help me with an experiment. I told him that the Bible indicated that the Spirit of God was working in the world to convince people of certain facts that had a bearing on the religious question. He agreed to answer a few questions that might tell whether he himself had already become convinced of these facts. I tried to stay away from Bible words in order to avoid any reaction which might be attached to such terms.

The first question I asked was this: "Do you feel that you have fallen short, that you have missed the mark in life, that you have broken the rules and failed to be the person you feel you should be?" "Yes, " he said. "I guess I would have to admit that." Strike one! The Holy Spirit had already been there to convince him of sin. Even though his awareness of sin was vague and self-centered, he was nonetheless conscious of his own imperfection.

My next question was aimed at understanding his concept of righteousness. "Do you think that there is an ultimate standard of righteousness, an absolute pattern of right and wrong or good and bad somewhere?" This question was a difficult one because recent philosophical trends have university students believing that all values are relative, that there is no absolute right and wrong. Nevertheless, this student responded, "Yes, I believe that our reference to good or bad is basically out of a concept we have that there is a perfect good, at least ideally." His answer was somewhat philosophical, but it still gets to the point. He believed in righteousness. He believed that there is an absolute standard. Strike two! The Holy Spirit had been there to convince him that somewhere there is that perfect standard to which we all look and by which we all must be measured.

My third question was fairly simple. "Do you think we will all one day have to answer for the kind of lives we live in this life?" His response was quick. "Yes," he said. "I believe that the afterlife, if there is one, will take its form directly from the kind of lives we have lived." Strike three! He had already become convinced of judgment. He would have hesitated to call these beliefs of his a conviction of sin and righteousness and judgment. Nevertheless, he did believe that he had failed to be the person he should be, that there is an absolute standard somewhere, and that he would one day have to answer for the kind of life he is living. What more is there for this young man to hear than the good news that Jesus Christ has died for his sins?

This awareness the Spirit gives to men is not as yet the conviction that leads to repentance. Merely to be aware of the *facts* of sin, righteousness, and judgment is not to be ready for a change. But when a person is confronted with the gospel he comes to see that his sin is not a personal problem only. It is a problem with God. Righteousness is a standard God intends to require. Judgment is a sure experience one must face as he stands one day before a holy God. It is not the same to admit casually, "Oh yes, I'm a sinner," as it is to cry out, "God, have mercy on me, a sinner!"

The fact that people are convinced of sin and righteousness and judgment is obvious in that they seek an answer to the question "How can I be acceptable with God?" Their attempts to answer this question may take many forms. But basically they will fall into the category of either the religion of man or the salvation of God. The young man I talked with, like many others, was repulsed at the idea that Jesus is the only way to God. It is characteristic of man to be offended at that idea. It is too narrow.

No matter if Jesus is the Son of God. No matter if he is the most remarkable character who ever lived. Man still does not like his absolute claims for uniqueness. Why is that? Is it because of some failure in Jesus? No. Most people are reluctant to call his character into question. No, the problem is that man is reluctant to admit that something radical must be done about his own sin. He hates the idea that there is nothing he can do to gain acceptance with God. He resents the total claim of sovereignty that Christ makes upon his life.

Every man likes to feel that there is something about him by which God will take notice of him, commend him, and accept him. We all hope to make some kind of ultimate and overarching sense of life, to feel we are living in a way that has value beyond the immediate situation. We like to feel that we have a workable, acceptable approach to life with which God is pleased. To accept the fact that Jesus Christ is the only way is to say that there is nothing in myself which can commend me to God. It isn't easy to admit that I am worthless, that I am totally unable to make myself acceptable to God by my own efforts. That is why accepting Christ is not a thing that comes out of the nature of man. It must be prompted by the Holy Spirit and the gospel message.

The Religion of Man and the Salvation of God

In his redemptive mission in the world, Jesus brought the salvation of God to man. Throughout his ministry he contrasted that salvation with the religion of man. A key statement of Jesus brings this issue into sharp focus: "Jesus said to him, I am the way, and the truth, and the life; no one comes to the Father, but by me" (John 14:6, RSV). In this familiar statement Jesus affirms, as elsewhere in the Scriptures, that he is himself the way to the Father. He thereby settles the religious question of acceptability with God. It comes only through the unique Son, for "salvation is found in no one else" (Acts 4:12).

The religion of man arises out of a deep-seated question which he has within himself. How shall a time-bound man get in touch with eternity? How shall sinful and unholy creatures such as we grasp hold of a holy God? How shall we, with all our imperfections and uncertainties, latch on to something which is perfect and dependable? How shall changeable and often unpredictable creatures such as we are latch on to a changeless and constant Creator? All of these are different ways of stating the same question, "How can a man be acceptable to God?"

I have wondered whether Jesus may have intended to point to three forms of religion in his reference to "the way" (hand religion), "the truth" (head religion), and "the life" (heart religion). Even though man thinks he has found a way, Jesus declared himself to be *the* Way. For all man's truths, Jesus is *the* Truth. Whatever man considers real life, Jesus is *the* Life. Whether or not Jesus intended these categories in his statement, he certainly rejected these forms of the religion of man.

Hand religion was the approach taken by the Pharisees in Jesus' day. He rejected this by insisting that the laws of God were made for man and not man for these laws. This hand religion or legalism had produced a man-made righteousness which God could not accept. At the same time Jesus insisted there was nothing wrong with God's law. The legalists had taken their eyes off their God and focused on his law. Though their outward behavior was apparently commendable, their inner life was unholy and dead. Jesus rejected this form of the religion of man and called its followers hypocrites. Their way would never do, for Jesus alone would give men the confidence of acceptability with God. Salvation would come "by a new and living way opened for us through the curtain, that is, his body" (Heb. 10:20). By focusing on the redemptive work of Jesus as our reference point, we can avoid the pitfall of legalism. We can refuse to be insulated from God by giving undue attention to his law. Paul wrote that "now a righteousness from God, apart from law, has been made known . . . . This righteousness from God comes through faith in Jesus Christ to all who believe" (Rom. 3:21-22).

Head religion was a second form of the religion of man that Jesus rejected. There were those of his day who thought of themselves as "a guide for the blind, a light for those who are in the dark, an instructor of the foolish, a teacher of infants" because they had in the law of God the "embodiment of knowledge and truth" (Rom. 2:19-20). In this intellectual emphasis they sought to gain sufficient knowledge and understanding to become acceptable to God. Jesus rebuked them: "You diligently study the Scriptures because you think that by them you possess eternal life. These are the Scriptures that testify about me" (John 5:39). In trusting truth itself they had rejected the truth of God. Again Jesus called attention to himself as the salvation of God.

The religion of man as heart religion is also rejected in the New Testament. Throughout the history of man there has been the tendency to want an experience with God which would prove he is real. These were the ones who came to Jesus asking for a miracle which would prove his authority. He responded, "A wicked and adulterous generation asks for a miraculous sign! But none will be given it except the sign of the prophet Jonah" (Matt. 12:39). Again Jesus focused attention on his own plan for salvation by predicting, "so the Son of Man will be three days and three nights in the heart of the earth" (Matt. 12:40). The immature Christians at Corinth were zealous of spiritual manifestations (1 Cor. 14:12), and Paul came to them "resolved to know nothing . . . except Jesus Christ, and him crucified" (1 Cor. 2:2).

The New Testament emphasis upon the redemptive work of Christ shows the salvation of God to be objective and historical, while all forms of the religion of man are subjective and self-dependent. Salvation of God is Christ-centered, while the religion of man is man-centered. The salvation of God comes out of the nature and purpose of the heavenly Father, while the religion of man is the product of the fallen nature of man. The salvation of God is dependent upon the power of the Almighty, while the religion of man is limited to the resources of human nature. The salvation of God issues in a godly attitude of self-giving, while the religion of man is but another expression of his self-seeking.

Taking a Closer Look: Religion or Salvation?

Let's take another look now at the three forms of the religion of man as they compare with the salvation of God in Christ. Let's address some key questions to each of these three forms of religion and also to biblical Christianity. The first set of questions: What is really wrong with man anyway? What is the weakness or deficiency in man that requires some kind of religious exercise to make him acceptable to God? Second: What is the basic nature of the needed solution? What is it that God expects and that man is striving to accomplish?

Third: What is the test of man's acceptability with God? What are the terms by which God will accept us? The fourth set of questions concerns the means by which man may become acceptable to God: What route should I take to God? What activity should I pursue? Fifth: Who is the agent by whom salvation is accomplished?

Who is the one who actually does the work necessary for becoming acceptable with God? I trust that as we raise these questions, we will be able to see more clearly the contrast between the religion of man in all its forms and the salvation of God in Christ.

Now to the first question, "What is wrong with man anyway?" The answer of hand religion is that man does not act right. His behavior is the problem. He does too many wrong things and not enough right things. Because he does not act right, man cannot meet God's requirements. Head religion disputes that answer. No, says the head religionist, what's really wrong with man is that he is ignorant. He doesn't understand. He doesn't have the knowledge of the truth that will set him free. Because he is in the darkness of primitive ignorance he cannot begin to understand God; therefore, God cannot communicate with him. But you are both wrong, protests heart religion. The real problem with man is that he is unspiritual and materialistic. His attitude is all wrong. Because of this he is unable to experience God and so will never be acceptable with him.

Now that we have our answer concerning what is wrong with man from these three forms of the religion of man, let's address the question to the salvation of God in Christ. We ask of the New Testament, What is wrong with man anyway? What is it about man that makes it necessary for something to be done in order that he may be acceptable with God? The biblical answer is that man is a sinner. He is a sinner by nature and a sinner by choice. The very root of sin is a self-willed rejection of the authority of God. Man has chosen to live his life without God. Therefore, his sin has separated him from God. He not only has the problem of a sinful nature that is hostile to the authority of God; he also has the problem of sins that result from that nature. These wrong attitudes and thoughts and actions further complicate his problem as sinner. The only way he can be acceptable to God is for this sinful nature to be dealt with decisively on God's terms.

The second question concerns the basic theme of these forms of the religion of man and of the salvation of God in Christ. What is it that must be established in order for man to be acceptable to God? What is the basic nature of the solution? Hand religion answers immediately that the solution has to do with moral duty. In order for man to be acceptable with God, he must fulfill his moral obligation through the keeping of the laws and rules that God expects him to follow. Head religion responds that the answer is in the area of knowledge and understanding. In order to overcome his ignorance and the darkness of his primitive mind, man must learn the truths and be enlightened in his understanding of the world, of himself, and of God. Heart religion says that the answer is in the area of an experience of the supernatural. Man must reach out beyond himself and his own material and earthly existence. Again, we note in these answers of the religion of man that the solution depends upon what man can do, whether through moral duty or knowledge or experience.

Then we ask of the salvation of God in Christ. What is the basic nature of the solution for man's dilemma? The Scripture answers that the solution is in a restored relationship with God. The emphasis is upon relationship. In Isaiah 59:2 we read, "Your iniquities have separated between you and your God, and your sins have hid his face from you, that he will not hear" (KJV). It was God's intention in the beginning that his relationship with man be open and unhindered by any tension or estrangement between them. But in deciding to make his own choices outside of the authority and care of God, man brought about a broken relationship which must be restored. The apostle Paul wrote that "God was reconciling the world to himself in Christ, not counting men's sins against them" (2 Cor. 5:19). So man's problem is sin, and his desperate need is for a restored relationship with the Father.

Of course, none of the approaches of the religion of man is adequate to deal with the problem of sin. Even though he does not always feel it, man is definitely guilty as he stands before God. Sin is not only a personal reality and a social reality; it is an ultimate theological reality. Sin is not only a transgression of one's own person and one's fellowmen; sin is a transgression of the will of God. For this reason, no amount of reexplaining or reinterpreting of sin will cause it to go away. It is a fact to which conscience continues to testify. It is a fact of which the Holy Spirit continues to convince man. It is a fact that every man must face. It is a fact that can be dealt with only through the blood of Christ, which cleanses us from every sin (1 John 1:7).

The Acid Test: God's Approval

The third question we ask concerns the test of acceptability. How can one know that he is acceptable? What is that one standard which separates those who are acceptable and those who are not acceptable with God? Hand religion says that the standard is righteousness. A man is acceptable with God only as he is righteous in fulfilling God's moral demands. When the point of judgment comes, his good deeds will be weighed against his bad deeds, and the result will determine his acceptability. Head religion responds that truth is the test. As a man has found the truth and embraced it and has settled in his mind the key ultimate issues of life, he has reached the standard which God expects. When he stands before the bar of justice and is asked why he should be allowed to enter into God's perfect presence, he will respond that he has found the truth and made it his own.

Heart religion responds that the test is spirituality. The only way that a man can establish his identity as an authentic person who is acceptable with God is through the experience of that which is beyond himself. When he stands to answer for this life, he will respond that he has experienced the reality of God in an undeniable inner grasp of the divine. A serious doubt remains, though, as we ask about the tests of acceptability. Can a person operating within the realm of the religion of man ever really know that he is acceptable? Will he not always wonder whether his performance has been adequate? Will he not always recall those points of failure which cause him to wonder whether he really has passed the test?

Let's ask the Scriptures what the test is for a person's acceptability with God. What is the test according to the salvation of God in Christ? The apostle Paul answers, "If anyone is in Christ, he is a new creation; the old has gone, the new has come!" (2 Cor. 5:17). Paul writes to the Christians at Ephesus, "You also were included in Christ when you heard the word of truth, the gospel of your salvation. In him, when you believed, you were marked with a seal, the promised Holy Spirit, who is a deposit guaranteeing our inheritance until the redemption of those who are God's possession—to the praise of his glory" (Eph. 1:13-14). So the answer is clear. It is those who are in Christ who are acceptable with God. In reality there is no one acceptable with God except Jesus Christ. He is the only one who remained utterly faithful, to the point of laying down his life that the purposes of God might be accomplished (Phil. 2:8). Therefore, it is only as we are in him that we are acceptable. In ourselves we can never be. But in him we are as acceptable to the heavenly Father as is the beloved Son.

We should also note that in the New Testament view, the fact that we are in Christ is a fact beyond our own experience. Being in Christ means that we are identified with him in all that he is and in all that he accomplished. That we were in him in his death on the cross means that our sins have been atoned for as he represented us there. Since we were in Christ in his burial means that our old sinful nature has been buried (Rom. 6:3). We have died to sin so that "sin might be rendered powerless" in our lives (Rom. 6:6). In his resurrection from the dead we were, in him, given a new life and a new nature. We can therefore count ourselves "alive to God in Christ Jesus" (Rom. 6:11). When he was received into heaven as the ascended Lord, "God raised us up with Christ and seated us with him in the heavenly realms in Christ Jesus" (Eph. 2:6). Since all that Jesus experienced gave him God's approval, I am approved of God only as I am in him. It is his experience and not mine that brings the approval of God.

The fourth question we will ask concerning the acceptability of man with God has to do with the means by which we become acceptable. What is man to do? Where is he to put his energies and attention and efforts to gain acceptability with God? Hand religion answers that man must strive in the area of his ethical and ritual responsibilities. He must fulfill all the requirements of morality and the ceremonies of religious duty. Head religion responds that man's attention must be given to the intellectual. He must concentrate on learning all that he can possibly learn. His energy, attention, and concern must be for grasping with his mind eternal truth, which is so elusive to man. Heart religion answers that the solution for man lies in his devotional life. He must leave duty, responsibility, and even thought behind as he reaches out for an experience of God. He must let his emotions guide him and concentrate on how he feels and what he experiences.

We address the same question to the Scripture concerning the salvation of God in Christ. Where must man give attention? What must he do in order to receive the salvation of God? This basic question of man's part in gaining salvation was raised by the jailer at Philippi when he shouted, "Men, what must I do to be saved?" Paul and Silas responded with one simple answer, "Believe in the Lord Jesus and you will be saved—you and your household" (Acts 16:30-31). Paul wrote further in Ephesians 2:8, "For it is by grace you have been saved, through faith—and this is not from yourself, it is the gift of God." So the answer from the biblical viewpoint is that man is to concentrate on faith. He is to trust God, to believe him, to rely fully on what God has accomplished through Jesus Christ and that faith is accepted for a right standing with God (Rom. 3:21-22).

The final question is this: Who is the agent by whom salvation can be accomplished? Who is the one who is depended upon for doing the work necessary for salvation? In response to this question all three forms of the religion of man are in agreement. Man is the agent by whom salvation is to be achieved. He is to lift himself by his own bootstraps. Though the emphasis may be on moral duty or knowledge or experience, it is still man who is to accomplish his own salvation through his own efforts.

When we ask the identity of the agent who is to bring about the salvation of God, the answer is clear from Scripture. Paul wrote, "But now in Christ Jesus you who were once far away have been brought near through the blood of Christ" (Eph. 2:13). The one who makes possible the restoration of the fellowship is Christ himself. There is no other. Man has no part but to believe. The efforts of man in his religion are but hindrances to his surrender to the finished work of Christ for his salvation. Peter made it abundantly clear in his sermon before the Sanhedrin. He said, "Salvation is found in no one else; for there is no other name under heaven given to men by which we must be saved" (Acts 4:12).

Immediately, the objection is raised that this is narrow and bigoted and certainly not to be accepted in a day of more open-ended approaches to truth and religion. But we are not the ones who came up with the idea. We did not just dream up the notion that Jesus is indeed the only way to the Father. Jesus himself said there is no other way by which a man may be acceptable to his Creator. We are only messengers who report the words of the one who by various signs and wonders was proved to be the Son of God.

Imagine that you are stricken with a fatal disease with no hope of recovery. Your doctor calls to tell you of a new drug which will cure your illness and promise life. Would you respond with some high sounding prattle about his narrow-mindedness? Would you insist that there must be several ways to cure the disease? I doubt you would argue that your way was just as good as his, that you were offended at his bigoted attitude. No, you would be delighted to submit humbly to his one remedy. The world today is cursed with the disease of sin. We can rejoice that there is an answer—if only one.

Let's review the contrast we have drawn between the religion of man and the salvation of God. The key points can be seen in a restatement of the questions we have just addressed to religion in its three forms and to the salvation of God in Christ. The diagram on page 38 will help us to see the whole picture at a glance. We are concerned with the nature of man's problem, the basic character of the needed solution, the test for God's approval, the path man is to take toward acceptability, and the agent by whom salvation is accomplished.

Religion—Pitfall for Evangelism

One of the problems we face in coping with the religion of man is the partial truth it professes. Who can criticize a desire for moral righteousness? The Bible requires this of man. Who can condemn a search for truth? Who can reject the desire for a personal experience with God? In identifying these emphases as the religion of man, we feel we are close to profaning holy things. But let's not allow the religion of man to hide its true nature behind robes of counterfeit sacredness. Let's not forget that the religion of man is still but a pious expression of fallen man's self-exaltation. Do not forget that man's religion still represents a false hope that somehow the carnal nature can be disciplined, educated, or spiritualized into a fitness for heaven. Nothing religion can do will atone for the sin of man that separates him from God.

A dangerous trap for evangelism is the temptation to present the gospel in terms of the religion of man. Many a Christian is attempting to live the Christian life in terms of hand religion, head religion, or heart religion rather than in terms of the salvation of God in Christ. They appreciate the fact that Jesus died for their sins, but they have

	Man's Problem	Solution Needed	Test for Approval	Path to Acceptance	Agent of Salvation
Hand Religion	Bad Behavior	Moral Duty	Righteousness	Ethical/Ritual	Man
Head Religion	Ignorance	Understanding	Truth	Intellectual	Man
Heart Religion	Unspiritual	Experience	Spirituality	Mystical/Devotional	Man
God's Salvation	Sin	Relationship	"In Christ"	Faith	Christ

never quite been clear as to their own part in the work of salvation. Could it be that this uncertainty is linked to a "religious" presentation of the gospel? Could it be that their counsel at conversion was in the terms of a folk religion that mixed the atonement of Christ and man's own efforts?

When a person is called in an evangelistic appeal in terms of moral reform, will his faith thereafter be attached to moral values rather than to the Savior? Will his interpretation of the Christian life also reflect a moral emphasis? If a new convert is called to make a commitment in terms of doctrinal accuracy, will he not then be attached to doctrinal values rather than to him who is the Truth? Will he see the Christian life in terms of right beliefs? What about the person who is converted in a call to an experience with God? Will his faith not be attached to experience rather than to the person of Christ? Will he not likely interpret the Christian life in terms of experience rather than relationship with God?

You may be asking, "Then are these 'converts' really believers in the true sense?" I don't think it's wise to lump everyone in certain arbitrary categories as we may be doing here and thereby pass judgment on their eternal destiny. I am not saying that those who misunderstand the basic nature of salvation are therefore unsaved. I am saying that we who try to proclaim the salvation of God to man ought to make it abundantly clear that "the righteous will live by faith" (Rom. 1:17). God, by his grace, has used a lot of poor preaching and witnessing to draw men to himself. But the vague presentation of a "religious" version of the gospel results in a misinterpretation of the Christian life. The evidence is all around us.

Take a look at the Christian who tries to live in terms of hand religion. He appreciates that Jesus has saved him. But now he knows he has a job on his hands—living for God. He sets out to get his old sinful nature under control. He wants to discipline himself for right living. He talks a lot about good and bad, right and wrong. His religion is based on a moral commitment to do certain good things and refrain from certain bad things. His conversion was almost a question of coming into a new relationship with moral values rather than with God. He has little enthusiasm for personal evangelism. His witness primarily concerns his ethical convictions.

Other Christians operate in their Christian lives in terms of head religion. Their struggle is to learn more and more of the doctrines of the true church, the true faith. They see the Christian life primarily in terms of standing firm in their right beliefs against the incorrect doctrine of others. They tend to break fellowship with those who have a different viewpoint. There is no room for open discussion and a respect for the ideas of others. They speak of the Word of God in terms which equates it with their own interpretation of Scripture. Their relationship to God is attached to their faithfulness to a particular doctrinal position rather than to God's faithfulness to them.

Heart religion is also well represented in some churches. These folks were likely called to an "experience with God." Their conversion may have been a particularly dramatic or emotional occasion. It is not difficult to see how a person might then begin to seek further experiences to give him security in his relationship with God. The reasoning goes something like this: "When God was there I felt his presence. Therefore, when I feel his presence he is there; and when I do not feel his presence he is not there." This kind of thinking leads a person into the trap of seeking an experience to assure him that God is still there. He may go from prayer meeting to prayer meeting, or from revival to revival, or from church to church, trying to find that experiential assurance.

In our descriptions of these "religious" approaches to Christianity, it is obvious that the patterns are familiar. But let's not begin to class every Christian we know according to these stereotypes. Our only purpose here is to draw a rather well-defined picture so that the tragedy of "religious" Christianity is clear. In any individual there may be a mixture of hand, head, and heart religion. But it is a sad thing if these patterns begin to crystalize. As a Christian grows older he may begin to judge everyone else by his version of the Christian life. He may become intolerant, or he may give up trying because he is unable to be "religious" enough. Either way, he never experiences the unity of the body's fellowship. He cannot really fellowship with those who do not see things as he does.

Those who take a "religious" approach to the Christian life cannot really rejoice in the atonement of Christ. They are not clear on its meaning for them. While they may understand the doctrinal confessions concerning the cross of Christ, they do not see it with the eyes of faith. The atonement of Christ for our sins is a remote theological idea. They may know that Jesus' death and resurrection make possible our acceptability with God. But they live as though God's approval awaits their best religious efforts. They are never really sure about God's attitude toward them. They may not be sure either about their eternal security. Their uncertainty may drive them to seek baptism a second or even a third time. They long to establish something definite in their own religious experience which forever settles their acceptability with God.

But how shall we call men to Christ in such terms that they will be attached to Christ himself rather than to morality, doctrine, or experience? How shall we make our invitation to men clear enough that they will exercise their faith in Christ alone and his atoning work? Can we present the gospel of Jesus Christ in such a way that men will be drawn to Jesus Christ? Jesus said, "But I, when I am lifted up from the earth, will draw all men to myself" (John 12:32). The eternal significance for the cross is yet relevant for our presentation of the gospel today. We will deal more fully with this gospel content in later chapters.

There is a place in our witness for a discussion of morality, for doctrinal argumentation, and emphasis upon experience. But these are side issues which must be brought into our witness only as they shed light on the simple message of grace and faith (Eph. 2:8-9). The good news the world longs to hear is not that they need to get their doctrine straight. It is not good news that people need to shape up their moral lives. The answer to people's lostness is not that they need to have a thrilling spiritual experience. The good news, the gospel of Jesus Christ, which the world today needs desperately to hear, is very simply this—"Jesus Chirst died for your sins. A way has been made in him for you to be acceptable with God."

So let's be narrow and like it. Let's boldly proclaim that God has provided only one way by which a man might be acceptable with him—faith in Jesus Christ. Anyone who tries to enter by another door is a thief and a robber and will not get in. All other approaches are but counterfeit fabrications of the religion of man. None of them can solve the problems of sin, righteousness, and judgment. Again, we must repeat that "salvation is found in no one else; for there is no other name under heaven given to men by which we must be saved" (Acts 4:12). To those who take a "religious" approach to Christianity, let us say with Paul, "You foolish Galatians! Who has bewitched you? Before your very eyes Jesus Christ was clearly portrayed as crucified" (Gal. 3:1). But let's be sure that we have clearly portrayed the gospel of the crucified and risen Savior.

The religion of man, then, arises out of the nature of fallen man, while the salvation of God arises out of the nature of God as a loving heavenly Father. The religion of man is based upon a man's speculation as to what is pleasing to God, while the salvation of God rests on what God has revealed as necessary for his approval. The religion of man is man reaching up by his own power to lay hold of God. The salvation of God is Christ coming down to seek out and save needy man. The religion of man has its hope in the wishful thinking of pious guesswork. The salvation of God has its hope in the unfailing promise of a faithful God. The religion of man pictures man himself as the hero of the faith in his struggle for God's approval. The salvation of God focuses on Jesus, the author and finisher of our faith, who endured the cross and is seated at the right hand of the throne of God.

Thanks be to God for his unspeakable Gift!

3
Leave Us Happy Pagans Alone

During a lecture series at a major university, an outstanding Christian speaker presented impressive arguments for the Christian faith. Interest among the students and professors ranged from indifference to enthusiasm, depending upon the opinions they already had. Obviously the conviction of the speaker was that everyone should be a Christian. At a question-and-answer session following one of the lectures, a professor well know for his mildly antireligious views stood to raise a question. "Sir, I am convinced after this week that you are indeed a Christian." The students responded with enthusiastic laughter at this friendly sarcasm. "Furthermore," the professor continued, "I believe you are happy with that condition. And I am happy for you. But what I wish to make clear is that I too am a happy man, though I do not choose to be a Christian." He paused as though reading the speaker for signs of understanding. "So, here's my question," he concluded. "Why don't you Christians leave us happy pagans alone?"

That's the kind of question which usually gets a reply something like, "That's a very good question." But let's go a little deeper than that and see if we can understand something of the attitude behind the question. Indeed, do you and I have anything to say to a happy pagan? What is evangelism to do about the person who frankly says, "Thank you, but I'm just not in the market for your product. Are we to respond in the way a zealous new convert did when witnessing to his co-workers: "All right, you guys can just go to hell if that's what you want to do"?

In the previous chapter we discussed the religious question and the answers to it given by the religion of man and by the salvation of God in Christ. We said that the religious question is "How can I be acceptable to God?" We said that those who attempt to find a solution to that question in terms of the religion of man do so through hand religion, head religion, or heart religion. We further asserted that none of these approaches to acceptability with God is adequate and that the only solution is the acceptability made possible through the atonement of Jesus Christ. Have we, therefore, neatly disposed of all philosophical barriers to evangelism? No, I'm afraid we haven't. We are yet faced with this fact: Everybody doesn't ask the religious question. There are multitudes of people today who just do not think in religious terms. They are those we often refer to as *secular man*.

Confronting secular man is one of the greatest challenges to evangelism today. If he is not concerned with the religious question or interested in his acceptability with God, then what do we talk to him about? If he doesn't ask the religious question, then what question does he ask? What is his ultimate concern? If he is not concerned about the problems of sin and righteousness and judgment, then what are his problems? Will we have to convert him to religion first and get him to ask the religious question before we can introduce him to Christ? Is there any way to get him to Christ without requiring him to be religious first? Why should we bother him anyway if he really is already happy? Why shouldn't we just leave all those happy pagans alone?

Finding the Unreligious Question

If secular man does not ask the religious question, "How can I be acceptable to God," then what question does he ask? Is there a secular equivalent to the religious question? Yes, I believe there is. In fact, we have already seen it in the comments above. The questions that man asks even when speaking in totally nonreligious ideas is this: "How can I find meaning in life?"

Of course this ultimate question in secular form may not be stated in terms of how to find meaning in life. In fact, it may not be stated at all. It may rather take the form of an unspoken and even unconscious desire to put the jigsaw puzzle of life together in such a way as to come up with a recognizable picture. One person may ask, "How can I be happy?" Another may ask, "How can I find fulfillment in life?" Yet another may ask, "What worthy purpose does my life have?" All of these questions are aimed at discovering some meaning in life. All of them really are asking, "What is the significance of the fact that I am, that I am alive, and that I am thinking about this question?"

We must understand that for the secular man, all these questions are addressed to a world without God. As we have noted, secular means nonreligious. In some people it may even mean antireligious. The secular man fully expects to find an answer for meaning in his life, if there is any answer, in the world as he pictures it. His picture of the world has no place for God in it. Of course, we recognize that there are degrees of this attitude. One person may have an extremely narrow secular view, even to the point of having deep philosophical convictions about it. On the other hand, one may simply have the view that he is getting along very well in a world without God; so why expect the difficult ultimate questions to be answered in terms of God?

I talked with a friend recently who had gone to great difficulty in an attempt to get a vibration out of his car. After five or six different sets of tires and a total of over a month and a half of time in the repair shop for this late model car, he had come to the conclusion that he'd have to live with the vibration. I jokingly asked whether he had considered the possibility that the car was demon possessed. We laughed at that because such an idea just did not fit into our understanding of reality. In the same way, we must understand that to the fully secular mind the suggestion that God might be the answer to meaning in life is utterly unthinkable. That idea may be a quaint and interesting superstition from the past, but it certainly does not fit anywhere in the secular understanding of reality.

So the nonreligious ultimate question may be stated as we have said: "How can I find meaning in life?" If we are to do the work of evangelism in a tangled world full of genuinely secular people, we must learn to deal adequately with this question. We must even learn to be sympathetic with the question. After all, it is a question very characteristic of humankind. All of us would like to think that life makes sense. Therefore, we all struggle to make some sense out of life. There are some people who never give it a thought or even a minute's attention. They live on the brutish level of mere animal existence. But for most of us, finding meaning for life is necessary for our own sanity. Otherwise we just can't live with ourselves. Even in those living on the animal level, the mere struggle to stay alive gives some meaning to their day.

We must recognize that man's search for meaning in life stems from the fact that he was created for a life full of meaning. Somehow he senses it, even unconsciously. Somehow he knows that it all surely makes sense. Somehow he believes that there are answers somewhere to the questions that plague his mind: Who am I? Why am I here? Where did I come from? Where am I going? What should I do with my life? Even though secular man may refuse to acknowledge God at all, the very questions he raises reflect a desire for meaning that reminds us that he was made in the image of God.

Happiness: the Supreme Good

Throughout man's history, he has debated about what element in life is the *summum bonum*, the supreme or highest good from which all other good things come. In most cases people think of happiness as that supremely good thing toward which all of life presses. Even the American Declaration of Independence speaks of the inalienable right to "the pursuit of happiness." Man instinctively pursues this elusive quality. He works to earn happiness, pays heavily to buy it, lays down his life to keep it, and weeps in despair when he loses it.

In a day of increasing freedom from traditional moral restraints, people let little stand in the way of their pursuit of happiness—any of these things are to be sacrificed if they stand in the way of happiness. Morality, responsibility, self-respect, loyalty—any of these things are to be sacrificed if they stand in the way of happiness. Marriage promises, business contracts, friendships, and parental responsibilities are all to be left behind if happiness calls. Happiness, then, is the popular equivalent to meaning in life. Without happiness life has no meaning.

The word *happiness* come originally from the Old Norse word *happ*, which means good luck. It is associated with chance, luck, or fortune. Happiness means good luck, good fortune, prosperity. It is a state of well-being and pleasurable satisfaction. The idea of happiness is related to happenstance, to what happens, to circumstances.

It is, therefore, attached to how things are going for you, how life is treating you. When things go well, happiness is intact. When events and circumstances turn for the worse, happiness is in danger of being lost.

I talked recently with a young airline stewardess and took one of my random, unofficial, and unscientific surveys. "What is it that gives you meaning in life?" I asked. She said, "Well, I'm happy. I have a good job, good health, and things are going well at home." She obviously was happy. But there was a wishful, cross-your-fingers quality to her answer. It seemed as though she expected something to spoil her happiness any minute. I told her that I had found joy and meaning in Christ that was not attached to circumstances. "That's good," she said. "It's up to the individual." She was saying two things. One was a sort of "you do your thing and I'll do mine." The other was "I've already told you I'm happy, so don't try to sell me on religion."

What can we say to a happy pagan who is apparently putting life together without God in a satisfactory way? First, we must be convinced ourselves that happiness may well not be the ultimate good in life. A good deal of contemporary evangelistic preaching is geared to the desire for happiness. The appeal stresses that God will give a person joy, help him solve all his problems, put a new song in his heart and a new spring in his step. Most testimonies emphasize how happy the Christian is because of all God has done for him. If a person hears these comments and sermons but considers himself already happy, it is reasonable to expect him to see no need for Christ.

God's View of Happiness

Is happiness the primary goal of God's will for man? We must answer that it is not. It is rather God's will that a person "be conformed to the likeness of his Son" (Rom. 8:29). In order for that goal to be reached, God chooses, calls, justifies, and glorifies men as his own children (Rom. 8:30). Man's primary problem from the biblical view is not unhappiness but unholiness. His worst enemy is not ill fortune but sin. Life is not to be measured in terms of happiness but in terms of victory over sin. Man is to seek not to satisfy his own desires, but to glorify God. It is not those who are happy but those who do the will of God who live forever (1 John 2:17).

Happiness is seen in Scripture not as that good thing to be sought. It is rather a result and benefit in the life of the one who seeks the will of God. Happy is the person whom God chastens (Job 5:17), for it is God who abundantly satisfies (Ps. 36:8; 63:5). Happy is the one who fears God and walks in his ways (Ps. 128:1), whose hope is in the Lord (Ps. 146:5). Happiness also comes from harmonious unity among brothers in the Lord (Ps. 133:1), finding the wisdom of God (Prov. 3:13), having mercy on the poor (Prov. 14:21). The New Testament speaks of happiness in the midst of trials and persecution (Matt. 5:10; 2 Cor. 12:10; 1 Pet. 3:14; 4:12-13). Happiness in Scripture is, therefore, a by-product of our being rightly related to God in trust and obedience.

How then shall we share the gospel with today's happy pagans? We must declare frankly that no matter how happy a person is without God, he is still answerable to God for what he does with his life. God has created man and has paid the supreme price of his Son's death to redeem him; therefore he lays an ultimate claim on each person's life. Happy or sad, like it or not, we are all responsible to God. Paul wrote that "the wrath of God is being revealed from heaven against all the godlessness and wickedness of men . . . For although they knew God, they neither glorified him as God nor gave thanks to him, but their thinking became futile and their foolish hearts were darkened . . . . They exchanged the truth of God for a lie, and worshiped and served created things rather than the Creator—who is forever praised" (Rom. 1:18, 21, 25).

As these verses make clear, the supreme sin is godlessness—living life without God, as though he did not exist. Rather than worshiping God as the center of value in their lives, men have "worshiped and served created things." This is secular man, refusing to worship God and glorify him. He rather gives ultimate significance in his life to the things God has made. John wrote, "Do not love the world or anything in the world" (1 John 2:15). Then he named the three "things that are in the world": (1) the cravings of fallen human nature; (2) the cravings of the eyes; (3) the pride of life. Let's look more closely at these basic approaches to finding meaning in life without God.

The first of these things of the world we may call the *pleasure* approach to happiness. It is the attempt to find meaning in life through the gratification of our earthy nature, the desire of the old man, the cravings of the flesh. The second basic approach we will call the *possessions* approach to happiness. This is the attempt to make sense of life by gathering all the things greedy eyes see and want. The third may be called the *position* approach, by which a person tries to find meaning for life in the vain and pretentious grandeur of earthly status. Note that each of these basic desires is a legitimate one that God recognizes as a human need: the need of pleasure, possessions, and position. The error is in giving ultimate significance to the pursuit of these created things rather than to the Creator.

As we have noted, there may be secularists by conviction, philosophical secularists who really believe life is best without God. But most secularists are only so by practice and not conviction. These practical secularists may well believe in God, but they live as though he did not exist. Their idea of meaning in life is attached to created things rather than to the Creator. We can even see many Christians whose pattern of life reveals that the most important question of value, purpose, and meaning are actually being answered without serious need of God. They have separated faith and life into two different categories. Faith involves the elusive and irrelevant world of religion. Life involves the reality of success or failure, gain or loss, joy or sorrow, meaning or despair.

The Pleasure Seekers

The most popular of the three basic approaches to secular life is the pleasure approach. In this, a person's primary aim in life is to be comfortable, to enjoy himself, to avoid pain or discomfort, and to strive for pleasurable experience. This is basically an effort to give in to the appetites of the lower nature. It is fully self-centered. As we have noted in chapter 1, the ethical motto of a permissive age may well be "If it feels good, do it." The person taking the pleasure approach has no better reason to get up in the morning than to spend the day in quest of personal pleasure.

During the economic recession of the mid-seventies, building starts were off dramatically. But in the first quarter of 1974 there was one type of construction yet unaffected by the recession—the building of entertainment facilities. The pleasure-mad world always has a place for entertainment. It is as though there were an inalienable right to be entertained. This activity may range from movies and spectator sports to active and dangerous pursuits like skydiving and hang gliding. Either way, the goal is pleasure. Either way the expenditure of time, money, and energy is indicative of one's purpose in life.

The pleasure principle for meaning in life takes many forms, but it is still recognizable easily enough. The acid test comes when a choice must be made between pleasure and responsibility. A man will forsake his marriage contract to pursue pleasure in an illicit affair. Parents will neglect their children for the pleasure of good times. A person will ruin his health for the pleasure of smoking or gluttony. No sacrifice is too great in the drive for pleasure.

I'll never forget a funeral in a rural town in which the most significant thing the minister said about the deceased was that he had been an avid fisherman. There was also the friend whose greatest delight in life was stock-car racing. Even though a nominal Christian, he made his choices according to the priority of his hobby. Another friend sought no such thrills. He wanted only to be quiet and comfortable in the pleasure of every evening at home before the television set. Such a variety these three presented; but each made pleasure his first priority.

The pursuit of pleasure, then, is a bondage from which Christ would set men free. Paul wrote that the person who lives in pleasure is dead while he lives (1 Tim. 5:6). He described the unbeliever as "foolish, disobedient, deceived and enslaved by all kinds of passions and pleasures" (Titus 3:3). The believer, like Moses, is to endure persecution if necessary "rather than to enjoy the pleasures of sin for a short time" (Heb. 11:25). His aim is to satisfy higher appetites, to seek God earnestly, his soul thirsting for God as he would for water in a dry and weary land (Ps. 63:1). It is God who genuinely satisfies the soul and evokes joyful praise (Ps. 63:5).

The Possessions Seekers

A second basic approach to making sense of life is in terms of material wealth. In this life-style, all of life is measured in terms of possessions. Values are ordered according to their worth in dollars. For a person seeking happiness this way, his very reason to get up in the morning is to increase his wealth. He looks upon all persons, opportunities, and decisions in terms of their potential effect upon his worldly goods. The pursuit of wealth becomes a deadly game of monopoly for keeps, a game which calls upon all of one's attention, energy, creativity, and devotion.

Shopping has become a favorite pastime for modern man (woman, teenager, and child). People are convinced that they can be happy if they can just have a new car, a new home, and more clothes. The ticket to everything is the credit card. A neighbor of ours was one of the restless, never-satisfied "shopoholics." Her daughter told us about one occasion when she had new drapes, new carpet, and new furniture in her living room. She sat down in the midst of it, looking around as though expecting these things to reach out to embrace her and satisfy her longings. Yet, unhappy, she whispered the deep sigh of boredom.

The whole value system of the possessions seeker is geared to things. He tries to meet every obligation and responsibility in terms of material wealth. He hopes to satisfy his wife with things instead of loving, cherishing, and protecting her as the queen of his heart. He may give his children everything they want and attempt to train them up in the gaining of wealth rather than in the building of character. He often sacrifices his health to gain wealth and then has to spend most of his wealth to regain his health.

It is not only the wealthy who are seekers of possessions. The amount one has does not reveal at all whether material wealth is that which gives meaning to his life. I have known men of middle and lower income who were obviously consumed with the desire for possessions. Their greatest delight was making a dollar. They developed a sensitivity about financial matters which usually surfaced no matter what a conversation was about. They delighted in their possessions, caring for them tenderly and devotedly.

Again, the Bible sees the drive for possessions as a bondage from which Christ would set men free. In his parable of the sower and the seed Jesus described the seed sown among thorns. He said that "the worries of this life, the deceitfulness of wealth and the desires for other things come in and choke the word, making it unfruitful" (Mark 4:19). In the parable of the rich fool, he dealt even more directly with the person who makes material wealth his security. He had God telling him, "You fool! This very night your life will be demanded from you. Then who will get what you have prepared for yourself?" (Luke 12:20). The Christian is rather to be seeking the reign of God and his righteousness in his life with the confidence that God will provide the needed material goods (Matt. 6:33).

The Position Seekers

A third approach to finding happiness in the world is the drive for position or status among others. Everybody wants to be somebody. Nobody wants to be nobody. The drive for respect, admiration, and prestige is normal to the nature of man. For some, though, it becomes the determining factor for meaning in life. It is for enhancing their position in the world that these people are motivated to get up in the morning. Though wealth and pleasure are often a part of this pattern, the true position seeker will spend all his wealth and sacrifice his pleasure to improve his status among men. His value system is arranged on the basis of power and prestige. The important people are the ones with power.

Vance Packard, in his book *The Status Seekers,* analyzes the drive for position in modern life. He shows how certain things, such as homes, cars, academic degrees, professions, and income all serve as status symbols. He even gives a chart by which you can rate yourself and discover your status level. The status seekers are most sensitive to their relative position among others as a barometer of happiness, success, fulfillment, and meaning in life. It is this position which gives them a security of identity and self-esteem.

We might think of movie stars and politicians as the seekers of position. But this malady afflicts many on the lower levels of the status ladder as well. A promotion at work, election as a club officer, moving to a better neighborhood—all of these desires will fit at almost any level of social prominence. The important factor is to see yourself as elevated to a higher position than those you think of as your peers. Even among street gangs of unemployed youth there is the clamor for status. Whether it is achieved by physical power, intellectual abilities, or material wealth, the desire for distinction and recognition can become man's idol.

The biblical view of this pride of life is clear. The psalmist writes that "the wicked, in the haughtiness of his countenance, does not seek him. All his thoughts are 'There is no God' " (Ps. 10:4, NASB). The writer of Proverbs says much of pride, basically that "everyone who is proud in heart is an abomination to the Lord" (Prov. 16:5, NASB). Pride is seen as the root expression of man's self-exalting rebellion against God. Paul described the position seekers who are found even in ministerial circles. "We do not dare to classify or compare ourselves with some who commend themselves," he wrote. "When they measure themselves by themselves and compare themselves with themselves, they are not wise" (2 Cor. 10:12).

What is the common factor in these basic approaches to a meaningful life without God? They are obviously "of the world" and are therefore condemned in the biblical view. They actually represent longings that God himself intends to satisfy. Though his primary purpose is not to make man happy, God does bless him with the riches of his grace when he can. For the pleasure seekers he promises a joy not attached to circumstances (John 15:11). For the possessions seekers he promises all the riches of an heir of God (Gal. 4:7). For the position seekers he promises to set them among princes and make them to inherit a throne of glory (1 Sam. 2:8). The risen Christ continues to call, "Come to me, all you who are weary and burdened, and I will give you rest" (Matt. 11:28).

Isolating the Secularist Virus

The difficulty we face in confronting a secular world with the gospel is that we may not be quite sure they need what we have. The pluralistic mind of modern man calls for an openness to all views and a reluctance to be committed to any one view. In this climate we may come to feel that secularism could be a workable alternative to Christianity. But this cannot be in the biblical view. The Christian gospel is the story of God's invasion into a secular world to find man where he is and reconcile him to himself. So secularism is not a new problem to God. Attempts to get along without God are as old as the Garden of Eden. But we must, since secularism is certainly a problem to us, understand the fundamental error that is in it.

Secularism actually arose in modern times as a corollary to the separation of church and state and the constitutional guarantee of religious liberty. Being free from a state-run religion, society finally came to be free from the real need for any religion at all. Having begun some eight hundred years ago, the movement toward the autonomy of man has come to a full expression in our time. As man has discovered laws to explain how the world and society function, he has come to feel he can exercise full control in science, social and political matters, art, ethics, and religion. He has learned to give adequate answers to all the important questions without bringing God into the picture. Apparently life goes on without God as well as it did before. Since it seems God cannot make much contribution, he is eliminated from more and more of the territory of life.

This is the root of secularism: the discovery that man can run his life fairly well without God. Rather than praying for rain, he irrigates his fields. Rather than praying for healing, he finds a medical specialist. Rather than praying for guidance, he consults the experts, takes a survey, and calls for a computer readout. Rather than praying for peace, he gets into Transcendental Meditation or consults a psychiatrist. Rather than praying for protection from his enemies, he develops more fearful weapons. Rather than teaching his children the truth of God, he teaches them that man is supreme. This ability to construct a fairly workable life without God is possible only because of the freedom God has given man.

Even with this apparent ability to get along well without God, modern man still suffers from his own creatureliness. He is yet at the mercy of disease, natural disaster, and the insanity of his fellowmen. He has yet to bring peace to a war-torn world. He has yet to find real release from the dark shadow of his fallen nature. No matter how proficient he becomes, his foolishness still surfaces to embarrass him. God has so constructed his creation that any concept of reality contrary to the biblical view will ultimately find itself moving farther and farther away from practical truth, from the way things really are.

Let's remember that secular man is still man. His nature has not changed. His basic needs have not changed. His apparent sophistication may give him a formidable look to the Christian witness. His seeming ability to find meaning without God gives him an aura of success and self-control. But no man has found what he longs for until he comes to God. Whether he is secular or religious is irrelevant. Christianity sees both secularism and false religion as empty counterfeits of the real answer found only in Christ.

Regaining Our Balance

What we must do in facing a secular society is regain a biblical view of the world and man. Dwelling on an analysis of secularism can tend to "fog us in" to a perspective too closed to be real. We must step back again and look at the whole situation from the vantage point of heaven. Though men think God does not exist and live as though he does not, the fact remains that he does. We must not allow the overwhelming skepticism of a secular age to brainwash us with a false picture of reality. When the secular skeptic draws a picture of all reality, he omits God. He has no need for God. The picture is complete without him.

We must repaint the picture with God in it and insist that this is the only version of reality that ultimately makes sense. We must not apologize for believing in God. The evidence is overwhelming for that belief. Read some of the recent works which set forth the evidence for the Christian view of the world. Let some of these creative and devoted scholars "load your gun" for you. In the academic community especially are needed bold, well-armed believers who will clearly and in love set forth the philosophical arguments for the biblical concept of reality. That, though, is not in the province of this book.

I am thankful that in our day God is raising up specialists in the area of apologetics, trained defenders of the faith who can help us meet the challenge of a tangled world. Let me say again that all of us will not become experts in the arguments and evidence for the Christian faith. But some of us must. All of us must work to equip ourselves with as much understanding as we can absorb of the arguments for the truth of the gospel. These arguments will not likely convince the person who chooses not to believe. They can be most helpful, though, to a confused seeker who is overwhelmed by the ideas of a secular age. Let's attempt to be ready to give an answer to anyone who asks a reason for the hope we have (1 Pet. 3:15).

Ours is the challenge of bringing the good news of Christ to a tangled world. We must not lose sight of the fact that no matter how sophisticated or skeptical or secular modern man may be, he is lost without Christ. His real need, as we have said, is not happiness but reconciliation to God through Christ. We must not let the issue of happiness divert us from the real problem. Whether a person finds some degree of happiness in the world does not change his position before God. As long as he continues his attempt at putting life together without God, he will remain estranged from him. As long as self is the center of his focus, Christ cannot be.

What, then, do we say to secular man? As foolish as it may seem, the most powerful approach we can make is to forthrightly declare the simple gospel of Christ. We must not apologize for it. We must not try to gloss it over. We must not compromise its astonishingly simple message. It is only the gospel which is the power of God unto salvation. It is only the gospel which will be honored to the maximum by the convicting ministry of the Holy Spirit. It is only the gospel which goes directly to the sin problem and makes an appeal to conscience. We must not be drawn off our own territory into endless intellectual speculations. We must insist on the truth and historical reality of the life, death, and resurrection of Jesus Christ in atonement for our sins.

To the intellectual we must declare the gospel. It is intellectually mind-boggling in its simplicity, yet unfathomable in its depth of meaning. To the skeptic we must plainly declare the gospel. We must not let his skepticism cause us to hesitate, for the only weapon against doubt and error is truth. To the secularist we must declare the gospel. It is the story of God's venture into a godless world to bring salvation to those "religion" had rejected. As questions are raised we must attempt to answer them. But let us not forget that conversion is not an intellectual transaction but a spiritual one. No amount of argument can persuade apart from the enabling ministry of the Holy Spirit.

The intellectual qualms and philosophical questions men raise about the gospel are usually a diversion from real objection. It is quite human to try and find legitimate arguments for positions we want to maintain. The unbeliever usually decides what he believes on the basis of his life-style. The primary objection to Jesus Christ is moral. Men do not object to his morals, but they reject him because of their own morals. A man senses that the claim of Christ on his life will require a moral change he is unwilling to allow. He also is offended at the implication he has something so wrong with him that he needs a Savior. Neither does he relish turning over control of his destiny to Jesus as Lord. So in order not to look so immoral, proud, and selfish, he sends out a smokescreen of intellectual arguments as to why he cannot become a Christian.

We must cut through the arguments to the personal dimensions of accountability to God. We must make clear that Jesus Christ has died for our sins. We must keep the choices in terms of the question "What, then, will you do with Jesus?" Every person who hears the gospel must face that ultimate and yet so personal question. Ours is to make sure he has the message straight. We must make sure he sees the issue of sin and the wrath of God. Sometimes man's intellectual powers make him drunk with pride to the point that he feels himself beyond God's authority. Once we make the gospel as clear as we are able, we must make the choice clear and seek to minister to the person through a time of prayer and decision.

Actually, the only people who really need God are the ones who are guilty of sin, who cannot control their own existences, who cannot avoid death. Man is yet a helpless creature in the face of eternity. No matter how much control man seems to have of life, he still suffers from guilt. He knows he is not what he should be. He still suffers from an inability to predict with any certainty what tomorrow will bring. So he waits helplessly like all the other creatures of planet earth while the irreversible gears of time continue to turn. He is unable to control the very stuff of which life is constructed. While he does all he can to stave off death, it slips in right before his eyes and snatches life away, to leave him weeping in frustration like a child.

Do we have anything to say, then, to secular man? Yes, we do! We declare to him the same simple gospel message we share with anyone else. We remind him of his own helplessness in the face of guilt, circumstance, and death. We point out that circumstantial happiness can satisfy only at a surface level. We remind him that he was made in the image of God for a dimension of life beyond these merely material values. We pray for him and love him and leave to God's Spirit and his Word the persuasion that is needed. In it all we know that not everyone, or even most, will respond in faith. But we do know that God is calling out a people for himself and that we must share the good news with all so that his sheep will hear his voice and follow him.

4
Repainting Ancient Pictures

Five-year-old Tracy leaned intently over the large piece of drawing paper. His stubby fingers gripped the crayon with the earnestness of a master artist. "Tell me about your picture, Tracy" came the musical voice of Mrs. Perkins as she stooped to examine his work. "I'm drawing God," was the serious reply. "Oh?" the unsurprisable teacher responded. "I don't think anyone has ever seen God. We really don't know what he looks like, do we?" Tracy didn't look up from his work. "You will when I finish my picture," he said confidently.

Drawing a picture of God has never been easy. Neither is it easy to describe the transaction which takes place when a man accepts Christ as his Savior. What words could we use to make a blind man see the Grand Canyon as he stands on its rim with blank, sightless eyes? What words could we use to make a deaf child hear the music of a mockingbird as he listens with still, soundless ears? What words can we use to make an unbeliever understand the miraculous spiritual business he can do with God if he places his trust in Jesus Christ for his atoning work on the cross?

The difficulty we face in communicating the gospel is that we must explain how the death of a Jew two thousand years ago is significant for the life of an individual today in this tangled world. What precisely is our message? Once we decide what our message is, we must decide on the terms we will use to communicate that message. We must make the abstract theological meaning of the atonement of Christ concrete and understandable for the life of modern man. We must make clear and specific the often vague and general connection between the cross of Christ and the conversion of a sinner.

The problem is further complicated because we must communicate the gospel in terms consistent with biblical truth and not leave wrong impressions concerning the nature of the Christian life. Out of the drug culture of the sixties came terminology such as "get high on Jesus" or "turn on to Jesus." There was probably little confusion among the members of that subculture as to what was being said. But these appeals lead a person toward an understanding of conversion and of the Christian life that is not true to Scripture. Trusting Christ for salvation is not merely a religious substitute for an experience with drugs.

In this chapter we will first answer the question "What is the gospel?" Then we will sketch certain biblical metaphors which help to explain the significance of the gospel for modern man. These ancient word-pictures were drawn by God's people centuries ago in an attempt to explain his mighty acts of grace in their behalf. It is our hope to use some of the same pictures to show how the historical event of the cross is clearly meaningful for modern man in his struggle to find meaning in life and acceptability with God.

Getting at the Gospel

Are we preaching the gospel or something else? From the time of the New Testament this question has been a crucial one. There has always been some confusion concerning the content of the gospel. Paul confidently preached the gospel of Jesus Christ, declaring it to be "the power of God for the salvation of everyone who believes" (Rom. 1:16). He proclaimed it through much of the Roman world. But he also referred to "a different gospel—which is really no gospel at all" (Gal. 1:6-7; 2 Cor. 11:4). This "other gospel" was a gospel of error that sought to add the work of man to the finished work of Christ.

Today we encounter numerous "gospels." These have included the "social gospel." This was the gospel of social redemption. The term has become a code word for some for a type of liberal do-goodism. Then we have heard of the "hot gospel." This usually means the gospel of hell, fire, and brimstone. Of course, throughout this century there has been a rash of cult groups, which have each claimed to possess the true gospel. Now we have been introduced in ever-increasing fashion to the "full gospel." This seems to imply that the gospel prior to the "full gospel" was either an empty or a less-than-complete gospel. Where in all of this do we find the truth of the gospel of Jesus Christ as the New Testament presents it? What are the elements of the gospel of Christ? How can it be discerned from false gospels? What is the gospel as it particularly relates to evangelism?

In 1 Corinthians 15 Paul spelled out as clearly as anywhere else in the New Testament the simple gospel of Jesus Christ. He told the Christians at Corinth that he wanted to remind them of the gospel he had already preached to them. He said that it is the same gospel that they had received by faith and had trusted to be true. He urged them to hold firmly to this gospel which brought salvation to them. He said that he had passed on to them what he had received and considered to be of first importance: "that Christ died for our sins according to the Scriptures, that he was buried, that he was raised on the third day according to the Scriptures, and that he appeared to Peter, and then to the Twelve. After that, he appeared to more than five hundred of the brothers at the same time, most of whom are still living, though some have fallen asleep" (1 Cor. 15:3-6).

The gospel Paul spelled out in this passage is the gospel of Jesus' experience here on earth. It speaks of his death on the cross for our sins, his burial in the earth, his resurrection on the third day, and the fact that he was seen risen by a great host of people. This is the gospel of Jesus Christ. Even at the time of the writing many of them were alive who could testify to these facts. It is actually but a simple narrative of significant, prophecy-fulfilling events in the life of Jesus of Nazareth. It is told as a matter of historical record.

Take a look at the elements we have noted in Paul's definition of the gospel. Notice what is not there. The gospel is not about what happened to the followers of Jesus except that they were eyewitnesses to the resurrection. It is not about the experiences of the church. It is not about the church in its struggles against the governmental and religious pressures of the day. The gospel is not even about the philosophy and teachings of Jesus. It is not about his healing ministry. It is not about the miracles he worked. The gospel is rather about those eternally significant events in his life by which he made atonement for our sins and was victorious over death in our behalf.

The significance of these events in the life of Jesus is at this very point: Jesus Christ provided in these deeds the needed atonement for man. Our English word *atone* comes from the phrase *at one.* We are "at one" with another when we are in harmonious personal relationship with him. Atonement, then, originally meant at-one-ment. In our modern usage we mean by atonement that process which removes hindrances to a right relationship with God. It was precisely this which Jesus accomplished in his death and resurrection. He took the necessary action to remove the barrier of our sin and restore us to fellowship with God.

As we have already discussed, the Bible assumes man's need for some atoning actions if he is to be right with God. It is understood that he is cut off from fellowship with God. He is totally at fault in the problem, for it is his choice to refuse God's will which has alienated him from God. This alienation must first be dealt with if he is to be restored to a right relationship with God. The sin barrier must be removed. The New Testament declares plainly God's hatred of sin. He refused to remove the terrible consequences he has determined will come of sin. But God's attitude is not a distant and uncaring contempt for the sinner. He does not turn away from man in disgust. He rather comes again and again, desiring to deliver man from the evil that is destroying him and separating him from God.

The supreme gesture of God's love and mercy is seen in Christ, particularly in his atoning death on the cross. Jesus came "to give his life a ransom for many"(Mark 10:45). Paul wrote that "we were reconciled to him through the death of his Son" (Rom. 5:10), for "while we were yet sinners, Christ died for us" (Rom. 5:8). We "have been brought near through the blood of Christ" (Eph. 2:13), for "God presented him as a sacrifice of atonement, through faith in his blood" (Rom. 3:25). Peter wrote that "he himself bore our sins in his body on the cross" (1 Pet. 2:24). In Hebrews we read that "Christ was sacrificed once to take away the sins of many people" (Heb. 9:28). It is clear that God does not forgive sin by lovingly overlooking it. He forgives sin because atonement for sin has been made in the cross of Christ.

The Cross Connection

Let's return, then, to the question we originally raised in this chapter: How is the death of a Jew in Palestine two thousand years ago significant for my life today? What is the connection between the cross and conversion? We can answer that Jesus died for our sins. But the question remains: How does that work? How did his dying actually affect me and deal with my sins? The best way we can attempt to explain this is in the terms used in Scripture to explain it. There are certain metaphors or analogies that sketch portraits of Jesus' atoning acts and interpret them to us in a way we can understand.

What is a metaphor? It is a word or idea which is pressed into service to give meaning to another idea by comparison. It is a picturesque idea with which we clothe a rather abstract idea to show it in a more understandable light. We dress a vague idea in an imaginative idea so that its features may be more easily identified. In communicating the meaning of the gospel in our tangled world, we must be able to explain its deep meaning in concrete, understandable pictures that speak to the modern mind.

The New Testament does not explain precisely how Christ was able to overcome the effects of man's sin and restore him to fellowship with God. But with a number of strong, graphic metaphors it does clearly affirm the truth of what he did. Some of the pictures describing how Jesus removed the sin barrier are these: He was the sacrifice for our sins; he was the Lamb of God; he gave his life as a ransom; he was able to satisfy the demands of God's justice; he "bought" our salvation. The atoning death of Jesus is beyond our experience and understanding. Since the fact of Jesus' death is absolutely unique, these metaphors are but illustrations and must not be expected to explain every detail. For our examination we will group the metaphors into three portraits of how Jesus' death on the cross deals with the sin barrier.

A Timeless Sacrifice

The Bible pictures Jesus as sacrificing his life to bring us to at-one-ment with God. This striking picture comes from the sacrificial practices of Judaism, in which atonement was connected to the slaying of an animal as a sacrifice for sin. Since the Hebrews believed the life is in the blood (Lev. 17:11), the blood of the animals had to be shed in the sacrifice. So the blood of Christ is often mentioned as of great importance. This does not mean the physical blood only, but the timeless benefit of that blood as Jesus yielded his life to God in complete obedience to his will. His death is called a "sacrifice for sins" (Heb. 10:12) and "a fragrant offering and sacrifice to God" (Eph. 5:2).

The power of Christ's death is associated with his perfect obedience to the Father's will (Heb. 10:7-9). He was "obedient to death—even death on a cross" (Phil. 2:8). This obedient willingness made the effect of his sacrifice complete. It was a sacrifice that did what the Old Testament sacrifices could never do, "because it is impossible for the blood of bulls and goats to take away sins" (Heb. 10:4). It was a permanent sacrifice, for when Jesus "had offered for all time one sacrifice for sins, he sat down at the right hand of God" (Heb. 10:12). So in willingly sacrificing his life, he canceled out the effect of sin. Not only did Jesus act as the officiating priest who offered the sacrifice; he was himself that sacrifice.

So the connection between the cross of Christ and the sin problem of man is pictured in this metaphor in terms of a timeless sacrifice that Jesus made for man's sin. Does this communicate to modern man? That is difficult to say. A child is drowning. A brother leaps into the water and rushes to his aid. In the process of saving his little brother, the rescuer loses his life. We understand the meaning of a sacrifice like that. A soldier on the battlefield throws himself over a live enemy grenade to shield his companions from the blast with his own body. We know what sacrifice means here. But the swimmer gave his life accidentally while saving his brother. Jesus chose deliberately to offer his. The soldier threw himself over the grenade out of instinct and training. Jesus planned his submission to the cross as the climax of his purpose of this life. The pictures we draw for modern man are only helpful to a limited degree. How can we explain the timeless relationship between Jesus Christ and all mankind? This is beyond us. It is a truth that lies in the fact that Jesus was a man in his death but at the same time the unique Son of God. This was necessary because only God could solve the problem created by man's sin. The soldier and the sinner both died of the same danger they sought to overcome for others. Jesus also died from the same evil which threatens man with eternal death—the curse of sin. Since God has determined that "the wages of sin is death" (Rom. 6:23), then sin must inevitably issue in death. In the cross the sinless Christ gathered all the sin of mankind to himself, and there "God made him who had no sin to be sin for us, so that in him we might become the righteousness of God" (2 Cor. 5:21).

A Costly Ransom

Another biblical picture helping us see the connection between the cross and our condition is the portrayal of Jesus' death as a ransom paid for man's release from the bondage of sin. Jesus said, "For even the Son of Man did not come to be served, but to serve, and to give his life a ransom for many" (Mark 10:45). The ransom Jesus paid for mankind was his own life. He placed himself in the hands of the enemy as a substitute for the captives of sin. Therefore Paul wrote to Christians, "You are not your own; you were bought at a price" (1 Cor. 6:19-20). He charged us further: "You were bought at a price; do not become slaves of men" (1 Cor. 7:23). Being set free from the captivity of sin, the believer must allow no force to take him captive again. He was released from the clutches of the enemy into the hands of a loving but sovereign heavenly Father so that now he belongs fully to him.

Can modern man understand this picture of Jesus' death as a ransom and substitute that breaks the bonds of our sin? Again, we cannot tell. A Japanese airliner is highjacked by extremists. The passengers and crew are threatened with death unless demands are met by the officials. After some discussion three airline executives offer themselves as hostages if the passengers and crew are released. Another situation: Irish extremists capture a British businessman and his wife in their apartment. Their demands are presented to police with the threat of death for their captives. A police official offers himself as a substitute hostage for the woman. This kind of ransom as a personal substitute is clear to modern man. It helps somewhat to clarify the meaning of Jesus' death in our behalf.

Having placed themselves in the hands of the extremists for the release of hostages, the airline executives and the police officials had done all they could. Their deaths would have served no further purpose. Neither did they have any choice whether to live or die. Jesus, though, gave himself over to the forces of evil for the express purpose of dying at their hands. He could have avoided death, but he chose to die as part of the plan. Peter declared in his Pentecost sermon, "This man was handed over to you by God's set purpose and foreknowledge; and you, with the help of wicked men, put him to death by nailing him to the cross" (Acts 2:23). It was, in fact, his death that broke the hold of the enemy on man. Paul declared, "And having disarmed the powers and authorities, he made a public spectacle of them, triumphing over them by the cross" (Col. 2:15).

Satisfying the Demands of Justice

Another portrait the Scriptures paint of how Jesus's death dealt with the curse of sin is the picture of Jesus accepting the punishment due for man's sin. God, as we have already noted, has made known to us the law that reflects his righteous character. God has commanded that man obey his law. Paul wrote that even if men do not have the written law, they are responsible for their sin because "the requirements of the law are written on their hearts" (Rom. 2:15). After making clear that Jew and Gentile alike have broken God's law, he said that "no one will be declared righteous in his sight by observing the law; rather, through the law we become conscious of sin" (Rom. 3:20). Then, "When we were still powerless, Christ died for the ungodly " (Rom. 5:6). Just as Adam's one act of disobedience allowed sin to capture every man, so also through the obedience of Christ many will be made righteous.

In Jesus' perfect obedience even to death, he satisfied the righteous demands of God. He overcame the power of sin by his perfect life. He overcame death by embracing it and breaking its grip on man as the dread result of sin. He overcame hell by the resurrection. He accepted the wrath of God against sin for all mankind and so took the atoning action that blotted out sin. Isaiah wrote centuries earlier of Jesus' perfect obedience in taking our sin upon himself:

> He was pierced through for our transgressions,
> He was crushed for our iniquities;
> The chastening of our well-being fell upon Him,
> And by His scourging we are healed.
> All of us like sheep have gone astray,
> Each of us has turned to his own way;
> But the Lord has caused the iniquity of us all
> To fall on Him (Isa. 53:5-6, NASB).

But we do not see here the compassionate Son appeasing the wrath of an angry Father. Rather, it is God himself who was "in Christ reconciling the world to Himself, not counting their trespasses against them" (2 Cor. 5:19, NASB).

Will this picture of the perfectly obedient Son accepting the penalty for sin in our behalf communicate to modern man? That is not clear. We do know that man normally believes that the lawbreaker should be punished. He thinks of payments as fair and necessary for an orderly society. He also knows that the innocent often suffer for the sins of the guilty. Children suffer for erring parents. The criminal's mother and wife suffer for his crimes. But taken together, these ideas are not quite sensible to modern man. It is difficult to think of one man taking another's penalty. Neither does it seem fair. Paul saw the same attitude in his own day. He wrote, "Very rarely will anyone die for a righteous man, though for a good man someone might possibly dare to die. But God demonstrates his own love for us in this: While we were still sinners, Christ died for us" (Rom. 5:7-8).

I'll never forget hearing a dramatic illustration of these ideas in a sermon some years ago. The story was about a rebellious young prince who ran away from home. His father, the king, was heartbroken. The elder son saw his father wasting away in sorrow over the loss of the younger man. To ease his grief he offered to begin a personal search in an effort to find the young prince. The father protested at first but then approved the plan. Month after month the elder son searched, hoping in every crowd, down every street, to see the familiar face of his erring brother. Finally one day as he entered a strange village, he found everyone rushing toward the town square. Arriving there with the crowd he discovered that an execution was about to take place. He overheard people in the crowd tell of a young man who had killed another in a drunken fight. The elder son was shocked to see it was his brother. After all this time, all this grief, was it to end like this?

Then to his surprise an official on the platform made an appeal to the gathered crowd. "Be it known that any man may now step forward to accept in his behalf the punishment about to be executed upon the prisoner." The elder brother quickly learned from those around him that this was a law in the town allowing any man to accept punishment in behalf of another. But certainly none would have any concern for this stranger. The elder brother pushed his way toward the platform. "I will do it, sir," he shouted. A murmur of astonishment swept through the crowd. On the platform the younger man recognized him. "Go home," the elder brother said. "Tell our father I have found you and sent you to him." The rebellious young man's heart was broken over his sins. He returned home a free man because of the one who honored his father and loved him enough to die for him. I suspect the story is fictional. Nevertheless, it captures our imagination with a portion of the truth of Jesus' death for our sins.

I have not dealt in a systematic way with the various theories of the atonement. But our purpose was not to describe alternative theological positions. Our purpose was, rather, to repaint these ancient pictures with a view to communicating the gospel to our tangled world. Whatever pictures we paint for modern man, let's make sure they carry the truth of the atonement of Christ. Because of man's sin he is separated from God and helpless to do anything about it. God took the initiative in sending Jesus to the cross to make atonement (at-one-ment). He died as the Son of God, deliberately, willingly, knowingly, on our behalf, in our stead. Having no sins of his own, he took all our sins upon himself. There he offered a sacrifice and was at the same time the sacrificial Lamb. There he demanded our release from bondage and was at the same time the ransom price. There he judged our sin and at the same time took the penalty upon himself.

> And being found in appearance as a man, he
> humbled himself
> and became obedient to death—
> even death on a cross!
> Therefore God exalted him to the highest place
> and gave him the name that is above every name (Phil. 2:8-9).

We have considered the biblical metaphors which picture how Jesus made atonement for our sin. Though many of these could be named, we have grouped them into three portraits of the work of the cross: (1) a timeless sacrifice, (2) a costly ransom, (3) a just penalty. In these, we were seeking to repaint the ancient understandings of how Jesus actually removed the sin barrier which separated man from God.

Now we will consider some biblical metaphors which picture the results of Jesus' atoning work in the life of man. They show in picture language what happens in the life of the one who comes to God through Christ. These metaphors are known theologically by the rather technical terms found in the Scriptures: justification, redemption, reconciliation, adoption, salvation, and regeneration. They are used by the biblical writers to describe some aspect of conversion and the Christian life. They are not applicable at every point to cover every detail of the meaning of the new life in Christ. They are often mixed in their use in biblical passages. Nevertheless, they each carry a distinctive idea, a particular way of describing the unique change in a man's life when he trusts Christ as his Savior.

To organize our thinking concerning these metaphors we will note several points about each one. First we will indicate the basic meaning of the metaphor itself. Second, we will show what each one pictures as man's condition of sin. Third, we will consider the nature of the change when man comes to Christ. Fourth, we will want to know about the resulting condition for the believer. After examining each of the metaphors along these lines we will point out the basic categories they may fall in and how they may be used in our communication of the gospel.

A Day in Court

The first picture is at home in a court of law. *Justification (diakaiosune)* means that God accounts or pronounces a sinner righteous. It means that God credits the whole work and effect of the atonement of Christ to the record of the one who believes (Rom. 3:25-26). The picture is that of a criminal before the judge in a court of law. The judge knows he is guilty. The defendant knows he is guilty. The demands of the law must be met. The judge, though, on the basis of a just punishment for the crime, declares that the penalty has been paid. The prisoner is to be accounted by the court as righteous. Even though he is morally guilty he is legally acceptable. Since the demands of justice have been fully met, there is no need for further penalty. The defendant is but to accept this new standing by faith.

The basic meaning of justification is to be declared righteous. The condition of man pictured here is that of guilt before God on the basis of his law. But that law has been perfectly fulfilled in Christ. In his death he accepted man's guilt and the penalty for it as his own. The result in the life of the believer is that he is accepted with God as righteous on the basis of Jesus' atonement. He is still guilty, but as far as the court of heaven is concerned the righteousness of Jesus is credited to the believer's account, giving him a righteous standing with God by faith.

Newspapers some years ago carried the story of a judge who heard the case of his own son. The young man was guilty of a drug charge. As he stood before the court for the disposition of his case, the defendant faced a stern judge. The judge pronounced him guilty and levied the maximum fine for his crime. Then he removed his robe and stepped down from the bench to pay the fine. This may illustrate somewhat the fact that God is our judge but also our heavenly Father. He declared the penalty for sin as death but sent his own Son to pay that price. Ours is but to trust him and be accepted as righteous by faith.

Bought and Set Free

The idea of *redemption* in the Old Testament is associated with property (Ruth 4). Money is paid according to law to buy back something which must be delivered or rescued. The word is therefore used throughout the Old Testament in the general sense of deliverance. In the New Testament the meaning of redemption *(lutroomai)* involves the idea of ransom. Men are held under the curse of the law (Gal. 3:13) or of sin (Rom. 7:23). The Redeemer purchases their deliverance by offering himself as the payment for their redemption. Peter wrote, "For you know that it was not with perishable things such as silver or gold that you were redeemed . . . but with the precious blood of Christ" (1 Pet. 1:18-19). Paul said that "in him we have redemption through his blood, the forgiveness of sins, in accordance with the riches of his grace" (Eph. 1:7).

In the biblical concept of redemption there are two results for the believer. First, he is delivered as from a curse which binds him or weights him down. Second, he is delivered to a fuller life of freedom. He is redeemed once and for all as he is released from the bondage of sin and death. But the progress toward a full life may be fast or slow according to the man. The constant factor is the direction he is moving by God's power—out of bondage into freedom. So the condition of man is bondage; he is enslaved. The work of Christ in atonement makes possible his release to a free life. He is bought with a price and gains the freedom that comes only in submission to God.

The parallel of human slavery gives many an effective illustration of the picture of redemption. I recall hearing the vivid story of the young black woman being sold at the slave market in New Orleans. She was but a piece of property, beheld with the regard men give an animal up for auction. As the price began to be called, the woman stood before the gawking crowd with her head bowed in shame. In the crowd stood a young plantation owner who was moved by the expression of humiliation and pain on her face. He entered into the bidding, raising his offer higher and higher until he was awarded the sale. When he went by to collect his property, he took the deed to the young woman and signed it over to herself, setting her free. She fell on her knees at his feet and wept in gratitude as she promised to serve him the rest of her life. Being set free, she willingly made herself a slave of her redeemer.

A Glad Reunion

The third metaphor we have named is reconciliation. Paul wrote of Jesus, "For God was pleased to have all his fullness dwell in him, and through him to reconcile to himself all things, whether things on earth or things in heaven, by making peace through his blood, shed on the cross" (Col. 1:19-20). The word *reconciliation (katallage)* literally means exchange, the establishment of a new relationship. Christ has done something by his death which makes it possible for God to offer peace to men. God has laid aside his holy opposition to the sinner and shows himself willing to bring men into peace with himself. He has found satisfaction in that great work of his Son and now calls upon men to be reconciled to him.

The basic meaning in this picture is that one person has been offended by the transgression of another. How well we know this condition—in family life, among close friends. Man is alienated from God by the offense of his sin. But God takes the initiative. There is nothing in God to cause man offense, so the offense is all from God's view. He cannot accept a restored fellowship with man until the sin barrier is removed. The first step is with God in the reconciliation which took place in his Son. At that time, man is yet a sinner and totally incapable of removing the offense. In the cross God moves to reconcile man to himself and enables man to respond in being reconciled. The result is that alienation gives way to restored fellowship. Paul wrote, "For if, when we were God's enemies, we were reconciled to him through the death of his Son, how much more, having been reconciled, shall we be saved through his life?" (Rom. 5:10).

Adopted as a Son

The New Testament metaphor of adoption is used by Paul to teach that in Christ God brings men into right relationship with himself and communicates to them the experience of sonship. In the Roman world a son was under the authority and control of his father almost to the degree of slavery. Adoption was the process by which a person was transferred from his natural father's power into that of his adoptive father. The legal ritual consisted of a fictitious sale of the son and his surrender by the natural father to the adoptive father. Thus, the adopted son gained all the legal rights of sonship and became an heir of the father's estate.

In the New Testament meaning, *adoption (huiothesia)* literally means placing as a son. It speaks of one being given the rights of adult sonship. Paul wrote that we were enslaved, but God sent his Son that we might receive the full rights of sons (Gal. 4:3-5). Because we are sons, he has sent the Spirit of his Son into our hearts to call out *"Abba,* Father" (Gal. 4:6). Just like the witness required at adoption proceedings, "the Spirit himself testifies with our spirit that we are God's children" (Rom. 8:16). Now we are no longer slaves, but sons. Since we are sons, God has also made us heirs (Gal. 4:7).

A tender story which illustrates this beautiful truth concerns a nine-year-old adopted daughter. Since she had been big enough to understand, the child's parents had explained to her that she was adopted. They saw no need for the secrecy which so often results in confusion and shock at later learning the truth. Then, as children will, some of her classmates began to ridicule the little girl for being adopted. Wounded and angry, the child came home crying. The mother so wanted her to see adoption in the positive and loving meaning it had for them as parents. She explained, "Honey, you are luckier than the other children. They had no choice about being in their families. Their parents had to take what they got. Your daddy and I *chose* you!"

Rescue from Danger

The word *salvation* simply means deliverance. But since it is the most often used word for conversion and the Christian life, it has become a technical theological term for the whole doctrine of salvation. In our study of metaphors, though, let's look at the simple picture it gives us of the miracle of a new life in Christ. In the Old Testament salvation meant deliverance from all that interferes with the enjoyment of God's blessings. It included rescue from natural plagues, internal dissensions, external enemies, or threatening conquerors.

For the individual, all the evils man faced were summed up in the word *death*. So the opposite of salvation was death. Since death and its attendant evils were worked by God's wrath, salvation was sought from this wrath. In the New Testament understanding, salvation delivers from everything that raises this wrath, above all from sin. Paul wrote that "the wrath of God is being revealed from heaven against all the godlessness and wickedness of man" (Rom. 1:18). He explained that "sin entered the world through one man, and death through sin, and in this way death came to all men, because all have sinned" (Rom. 5:12). Sin, then, has man in its grip. He is in danger of death because of sin.

Salvation pictures the sinner in the grips of sin like a swimmer drowning in clutching waters. He is helpless to free himself. All he can do is cry out for help. But through the victory won at the cross, the power of sin and death is broken. God has come in Christ to "seek and to save" those who are lost. Rather than going down to death those who believe will not perish but have everlasting life (John 3:16). A drowning swimmer, a victim of terminal disease, a lost and starving camper—any modern picture of the rescue of someone in peril of death may help communicate a part of what the Bible means by salvation.

A New Beginning

The last metaphor we will sketch is *regeneration*. Though this word *(palingenesia)* occurs only twice in the New Testament, the idea of a new birth is throughout. The most familiar discussion of the need for man to be born again is probably in Jesus' conversation with Nicodemus (John 3). Here we see that even the most faithfully religious of men is spiritually dead and is therefore unable to live up to the demands of God. He must have a birth of spiritual life if he is to do God's will. Man has fallen from the plane of the spiritual and lives on a merely earthy level, but by being "born again" he can live the spiritual life that God requires.

This new birth comes by the presence of the Holy Spirit on the basis of the atonement of Christ. Jesus asserted that "the Spirit gives life; the flesh counts for nothing" (John 6:63). Paul wrote that God saves us "by the washing of regeneration and renewing by the Holy Spirit" (Titus 3:5, NASB). Though once dead in transgressions and sins, the believers have been made alive with Christ (Eph. 2:5). This change is so radical Paul could speak of a "new creation" (2 Cor. 5:17), a "new self, created to be like God in true righteousness and holiness" (Eph. 4:24). So Peter compared the believers to "newborn babies" (1 Pet. 2:2); they have been born again (1 Pet. 1:23).

Most of us have from time to time longed for a new beginning, a chance for a fresh start. Our history haunts us with mistakes. This desire to leave all that behind finds thousands of apparently responsible people disappearing each year and abandoning family, friends, and careers. Many a story has surfaced of those who have tried to make new beginnings, establish new families, start new lives. But in all these attempts they are yet the same people. What the Bible speaks of is not new surroundings without but a new life within. Only through the atoning work of Christ is that new life possible, for because "Christ was raised from the dead through the glory of the Father, we too may live a new life" (Rom. 6:4).

As we have already indicated, these biblical metaphors are not given in Scripture as systematic and fully developed explanations of the new life in Christ. They are rather pictures, like snapshots that catch the subject at a particular angle, with a particular expression, or in a particular light. Each of these analogies seeks to describe the same thing, the results of Jesus' atoning work in the life of the believer. Yet none of them fully describes it. One metaphor may stress one feature, while another emphasizes some other. We must take care not to press them too far in their application. Like the parables of Jesus, they do a good job of making their point. But they should not be asked to speak much beyond that.

It might be helpful to note that some of these metaphors tend to focus on the new *position*, or standing with God a person has in Christ. Justification probably pictures this heavenward emphasis most clearly. It sees the spiritual transaction as fully beyond our experience. Another emphasis is upon *relationship* and pictures the new life in terms of a new connection which has been established between man and God. Reconciliation is a good example of this, picturing us as restored to fellowship with God. This relational emphasis seems to hover between heaven and earth, between the divine reality fully beyond us and the experiences in life so close at hand. A third focus for the metaphors is upon the *transformation* of the man in Christ in his own life. Regeneration well represents this emphasis. The new birth seems to be more of an "experience" than any of the other metaphors. The following diagram indicates these different emphases as they range between the objective and the subjective, that which is fully beyond us and that which is part of our experience.

Emphasis	Metaphor	Man's Condition	Change	Result
Position	Justification Redemption	guilty in bondage	declared right ransomed	righteousness freedom
Relationship	Reconciliation Adoption	estranged orphaned or enslaved	restored adopted	fellowship sonship
Transformation	Salvation Regeneration	emperiled dead	rescued born again	safety eternal life

It is also interesting, in summary, to look at a composite picture of the benefits of the atonement of Christ. All the metaphors together give a graphic portrait of the sinner before God. He is guilty of sin, in bondage to the power of sin, estranged from God, orphaned or enslaved, threatened with death, and, indeed, spiritually dead. But because of the cross of Christ he is declared righteous, ransomed from bondage, restored to fellowship with God, adopted as a son, rescued from the threat of death, and born again. As a result, the believer is acceptable to God as righteous, free to become all God purposes for him, in close unhindered fellowship with God, a son and heir to his riches, safe forever from the threat of death, and really alive with resurrection life. Amen? Amen!

Drawing a picture of God has never been easy. Neither is it easy to describe how Jesus removed the barrier between man and God and what that means for us today. Nevertheless, we can know that God does not leave us without a way of describing what it means to be a Christian. The ancient pictures given us in Scripture can be repainted in such a way that modern man may see what God has done in Christ. Again, let us be able to say about our witness what Paul did about his, "Before your very eyes Jesus Christ was portrayed as crucified" (Gal. 3:1).

5
A Faith that Looks Before It Leaps

"Who can tell me what *faith* means?" asked Mrs. Grimes. It was a Sunday School class of bright-eyed first graders. "I can, I can," the reply came with enthusiasm. "All right, Janie, you tell us." The little girl spoke with the voice of experience, "Faith is what you need in the dark when you are afraid." "I know," came another response, "faith is what you have to be a missionary." "Does anyone else know what faith is?" Mrs. Grimes probed for another answer. "I know," one of the bus children responded, "faith is when you believe what you know ain't true."

That last answer has a familiar ring to it. "Faith is when you believe what you know ain't true." Most of us would have to confess that faith is a mystery to us. We read in the Bible of those who had great faith, and we wonder how it might feel to be able to trust God like that. We read of missionaries, preachers, and great Christians of the past who have demonstrated outstanding faith. We are envious of them because it seems so difficult to muster enough faith even to expect a prayer to be answered, much less to live totally by faith, as some of the heroes of the past have done.

In the work of evangelism faith is of special importance. We have already said that faith is the one response on man's part which makes possible a right relationship with God. As we preach the gospel, then, it is a response of faith that we seek. But what kind of faith is necessary for conversion? How much faith does a person need to have before he can actually be saved? Since faith is necessary to salvation, what can be done about the person who has too little faith? How can we help someone to have greater faith?

Leaping into the Dark

The challenge we face today in understanding biblical faith is that the prevailing philosophical idea of faith is not what the Bible presents faith to be. Existentialism has colored the thinking of our tangled world to the point that modern man is affected by this philosophy without even realizing it. In this way of thinking, faith has no relationship whatever to the rational or the logical. Faith does not have to be reasonable or make sense; in fact, it cannot. In this view the things that would have to do with our discussion—God, purpose in life, values, love, the supernatural—are not probable. No amount of evidence can prove them real or true. Since these things cannot be proved, they are discussed in a category that does not require any proof or evidence. This is the category of the nonrational and nonlogical. So thinking and reasoning are to be left behind when discussing God, purpose in life, and salvation.

Since God and my relationship with him are not the kinds of things that can be reasoned out or understood in terms of evidence, how can I even talk about these things? How can God be real and meaningful to me? How can I find purpose and meaning in life if there's no way to discuss it rationally? The answer given by existentialism is to leave your reasoning and logic behind and take a leap of faith into the nonrational and nonlogical realm. So faith has nothing to do with knowledge, evidence, fact, reasonableness, or logic. Faith has to do with leaping into the unknown and leaving all reason behind.

This kind of thinking leads to the conclusion that it doesn't matter whether Jesus actually ever lived. People who follow this thinking believe that the Jesus of history is not important. What is important is the Christ of faith, who cannot be proved or verified—only experienced in the realm beyond the rational and logical. Many people today tend to choose the mystical Christ apart from the historical roots of his earthly life. They can make Christ to be anything they like. He becomes but a projection of their own ideas flashed on the screen of heaven. No one can question their ideas about God because there is no evidence for it. The God presented in the Bible is optional. Every person's faith is authoritative in itself.

As we have said, modern man has been influenced by this kind of thinking without even realizing it. He has come to put faith in the category of the unthinking and nonlogical. Faith does not need to make sense. It is just faith. This type of thinking finds man straining to believe the unbelievable, trying to make sense out of what makes no sense, reaching out from the logical, rational, reasonable world to make a leap into the space beyond. The aim is to have an experience that is authentic, an experience of the order that makes your own life meaningful.

I read recently an interesting statement in a book of quotations: "Faith is but a step in the dark onto the rock that is Christ." This sounds good at first because it expresses what we have come to believe that faith is. It sounds like there is something solid and especially religious about stepping out into the dark in an irrational, illogical step that to the normal, reasonable way of thinking would be totally meaningless. This, for much of modern thinking, is what we mean by faith. It is a leap into the dark unknowable and unknown. It is reaching out beyond what makes any sense at all to the mind of man to believe the unbelievable.

When we call for faith in our tangled world, people may respond that they already have faith and that their faith is just as good as ours. Since faith requires no evidence and has nothing whatever to do with reasonable thinking, one person's faith is just as good as another's. No particular message need be involved. No particular truth need be involved. In fact, *truth* is not a word that can even be connected with faith. Faith is something that goes beyond the idea of truth. It is something that has more to do with experience that reaches out beyond oneself and leaves any concept of truth, right or wrong, good or bad, logic or reason, behind.

Another response to our call for faith may be that faith is stupid. Anything that cannot be proved true should not be believed. Because there is no way to prove the things that we are calling for one to believe, then it is foolish to believe it. This response equates Christian faith with existentialist faith and comes to the conclusion that any kind of faith is nonsense double-talk about believing what really isn't true. When we say *faith* from the biblical viewpoint, we have one thing in mind; but modern man hears us say *faith* and understands that word to mean something else altogether.

Since faith is the one necessary response that opens a person for salvation, it is vital that we understand it. We will consider, then, several key biblical teachings about faith as they relate to evangelism. Our purpose is not so much to set out a doctrine of faith as it is to understand how faith works. We are to call on men to believe. This is our basic evangelistic appeal: "Believe in the Lord Jesus, and you will be saved" (Acts 16:31). If faith is that single response we seek, then let's be as clear as possible about biblical faith.

Defining What Faith Is

The Bible makes clear that God has so ordered his dealings with men that there is no way a person can be rightly related to him except by faith. Anyone who comes to God must believe that he is and that he is a rewarder of those who seek him (Heb. 11:6). Any person who would be rightly related to God can be so only through a confidence and trust in him. Faith is that which adjusts man to a new way of living and thinking from God's viewpoint. Faith is a person's one possible receptive attitude toward God. It is the attitude in which he realizes that he brings nothing worldly to his relationship with God in order that he may receive from God everything necessary for that relationship.

Where the word *faith* is used in the New Testament, there are two basically different meanings. On the one hand is the rather passive meaning of fidelity or trustworthiness. On the other hand is the active meaning of faith or trust. In the vast majority of cases in the New Testament, faith *(pistis)* means reliance or trust, the active response rather than the passive. Faith, then, is not merely a passive attitude of receptivity. It is rather a deliberate reaching out to place trust and confidence in God.

The best-known New Testament definition of faith is found in Hebrews 11:1. The familiar King James translation of that verse is, "Now faith is the substance of things hoped for, the evidence of things not seen." To clarify the meaning, let's think of faith in action terms and rephrase the definition like this: "Faith gives substance to the things hoped for and makes visible the things not seen." What is substance? Substance is that which has material reality to it. It is actual and measurable; it can be seen, touched, tasted, smelled, or heard. So faith makes real in our own experience those things which are hoped for.

What are the things hoped for? The things hoped for are the

things God has promised in his Word. When he seeks answers for his deepest problems, man has little reason to hope for anything beyond what God has promised. Faith is that which makes real and actual to man the things God has promised. In no other way are the promised blessings of God released to man than by faith. Neither has man any hope of receiving from God anything other than what he has promised.

Faith also makes visible the things not seen. What are these unseen things? They are the realities of the spiritual realm. No man has seen God (John 1:18). Neither can we see the Spirit of God among us or the mighty hosts of God arrayed against the forces of evil. But by faith our eyes are opened to the spirit world. We are enabled by the Spirit of God to see what otherwise would remain unseen (1 Cor. 2:9-10). So faith makes the promises of God real and the spiritual realm visible so that an entirely new dimension of life is opened to the one who believes God.

A Reasonable Faith

We often talk about faith in quantitative terms, as a matter of having a great amount of faith or a small amount of faith. This seems to fit with the Bible understanding of faith. Jesus remarked about those with great faith and at other times rebuked some for having little faith. But modern man thinks of the person with great faith as the one who has the unusual ability to leap farthest into the dark. He is the person who can actually sincerely believe what is most absurdly unbelievable. But is this the biblical understanding of faith? Let's examine some of the passages that might guide us at this point.

In Matthew 15:21-28 is the story of the Canaanite woman who came to Jesus asking that her daughter be healed. Jesus ignored her at first. As she continued to cry after him, he told the woman he had been sent to the Jews. He explained that the food provided for the children was not to be given to the dogs. He was referring to the Jews' view of Gentiles as "dogs." This seems like a harsh statement and difficult for us to understand in light of the compassion of Jesus. But the woman evidently understood it. She said that the dogs **were** at least given the crumbs from the table of their master.

Jesus was amazed at her great faith. He responded by healing her daughter. We are also amazed because her statement does not seem to reveal any great faith. It looks more like she made a wisecrack to Jesus. What we need to see here, though, is that this woman understood something of the sovereignty of God. She saw that God in his sovereignty had chosen Israel. Jesus was obedient to that sovereign choice of God in choosing Israel and rejecting, at least at this moment, the needs of the Canaanites. The point was that she understood something about God rather than that she had a great ability to believe the unbelievable.

The other instance where Jesus remarked about great faith had also to do with a Gentile (Matt. 8:5-13). This man came to Jesus asking for healing for his servant. He was a Roman military man who told Jesus he also was a man under authority and had those who were under his authority. He could command one to go, and he went; another to come, and he came. He said to Jesus, "All you need to do is to say the word, and my servant will be healed." Jesus commented about the great faith this man had. Yet this soldier seems to us to be a very practical man. He certainly does not appear to be a mystic any more than the Canaanite woman. The point we observe again is that he understood something about God.

This military man understood the authority structure under which Jesus was operating. He understood that Jesus was one in authority who could deal with the evil forces of demonic possession, disease, or even death by just a word of command. He understood that Jesus exercised the very power of God. He understood something about the fact that Jesus himself was fully and totally submissive to the authority of God and that this fact qualified him to speak with the authority of God. Again, this man was not blessed with an unusual ability to believe the unbelievable; rather, he had an unusual insight into the nature of God, his purpose, and his way of operating.

There are several instances in the New Testament in which Jesus rebuked the disciples or the people around him for their little faith. What did Jesus mean when he talked about little faith? As we analyze these passages, we see that he was really talking about a poor understanding of the nature of God and his way of working. Faith is not a product of some virtue in man. It is a response to understanding. In the New Testament view faith requires evidence, is rational and logical, and definitely makes sense

We remember the story of Jesus allowing Peter to walk on the water (Matt. 14:25-33). As Peter began to sink, Jesus stretched forth his hand, caught him, and said to him, "You of little faith. Why did you doubt?" The problem was not with the quantity of Peter's faith—that is, how much faith he had. The problem at this point was with the understanding Peter had as to the source of his ability to walk on the water. Peter at first was concentrating on Jesus as the source of his power. He understood that with Jesus this ability was not an unbelievable impossibility. As he began to walk on the water, believing indeed that it was Jesus who was enabling him to do so, he was successful with it. But as he turned to notice the wind and to remember how impossible such a feat is to a man, he began immediately to sink.

The point was not that he had lost through some kind of leakage the great amount of faith he began with. The point was that he had taken his eyes off the source of enabling which allowed him to walk on the water. He began with an apparent confidence, a childlike trust in the ability Jesus had to bid him come on the water and enable him to walk, He failed to keep in mind the reasonableness of walking on the water at Jesus' command. He began to think about the wind, about himself, and about how unthinkable it is for a man to walk on the water.

Peter actually moved from thinking it reasonable to walk on the water to thinking the reverse. He moved away from a consideration of the evidence: (1) that Jesus was able to walk on the water; and (2) that Jesus had commanded him to walk on the water. He moved from this reasoning based on the evidence at hand and the logical assumptions which might follow from it to a kind of thinking which said it is totally unreasonable to walk on the water, even though the evidence for Jesus' ability to make it happen was overwhelming. Peter probably began trying to muster his ability to believe the unbelievable. He failed.

Another instance of Jesus' rebuking the disciples because of their little faith is recorded in Matthew 16. On this occasion Jesus and the disciples were crossing the lake in a boat, and the disciples discovered that they had forgotten to take bread. About that time Jesus told them to be on their guard against the yeast of the Pharisees and Sadducees. Misunderstanding what he said, they discussed among themselves whether he said this because they hadn't brought any bread. Aware of this discussion, Jesus asked, "You of little faith, why are you talking among yourselves about having no bread? Do you still not understand? Don't you remember the five loaves for the five thousand, and how many basketfuls you gathered? Or the seven loaves for the four thousand, and how many basketfuls you gathered? How is that you don't understand that I was not talking to you about bread?" (Matt. 16:8-11).

It is interesting to note what Jesus did in this passage in rebuking the disciples for their little faith. First he asked them, "Do you still not understand?" He was equating little faith and lack of understanding. The reason they had so little faith is because they did not yet understand about his ability to deal with any situation which might arise. A second thing Jesus did was to review the evidence with them that their failure to bring bread along on the trip was of no consequence. He reminded them of the five loaves that fed five thousand and of how many basketfuls of leftovers they had gathered. He reminded them that seven loaves fed four thousand and of how many basketfuls they had gathered. In reviewing this evidence, Jesus was indicating that there was sufficient reason for them to trust him in the matter of bread, that their faith could well rest on that evidence. Some commentators indicate that the reason Jesus instructed the disciples to pick up all of the leftovers in the feeding of those multitudes was that they might never forget the experience.

We remember Thomas, who is called the doubter. When Thomas joined them in worship, the other disciples told him that they had seen the Lord. But he said, "Unless I see the nail marks in his hands and put my finger where the nails were, and put my hand into his side, I will not believe it" (John 20:25). When Jesus appeared a week later and Thomas was there, he did not rebuke Thomas for this kind of doubt. Jesus rather said to him, "Put your finger here; see my hands. Reach out your hand and put it into my side" (John 20:27). Jesus did not rebuke him for refusing to believe when there was no evidence at hand. He rather presented him hard evidence as to why he should believe and then said, "Stop doubting and believe" (John 20:27). Thomas answered, "My Lord and my God" (John 20:28).

Jesus also stated to Thomas, "Because you have seen me, you have believed; blessed are those who have not yet seen and yet have believed" (John 20:29). Here Jesus was referring to those who believed on the basis of eyewitness testimony, even though they did not personally see him as Thomas did. Believers of today fall into that category. God has provided us the testimony of faithful men who have reported to us in Scripture what took place. This kind of evidence has a high degree of dependability, especially when heard from four different eyewitnesses. John wrote that Jesus did many other miraculous signs not recorded in his report. "But these are written," he said, "that you may believe that Jesus is the Christ, the Son of God, and that by believing you may have life in his name" (John 20:31).

We could examine more passages at this point. But it seems clear from those we have looked at that the New Testament concept of faith is not a matter of believing the unbelievable, of plunging into darkness in a senseless rejection of reason and logic. Biblical faith is based on evidence. Throughout history God has chosen to bare his mighty arm to demonstrate his power and faithfulness to his people. These demonstrations of God's presence and power are evidence of his trustworthiness even today.

In the old Testament as well as the New Testament, the hymns of praise and sermons of admonition are usually recountings of the evidence of God's faithfulness in the lives of his people. Biblical faith does not say believe anyway, but believe because. In preaching the gospel to modern man, we do not offer him unbelievable speculation. We bring him the facts of the life, death, and resurrection of Jesus Christ and call upon him to believe that God has worked this mighty redemptive work in his behalf.

Where Faith Begins

How much faith do you have? This kind of question causes most of us to answer, "I don't know, but I'm sure it's not nearly enough." Like checking the oil in our cars, we want to pull our spiritual dipsticks and check the faith level in our hearts. But by checking in my heart to see about my faith, I am looking in the wrong place. Faith begins with God and his Word. Paul wrote, "Faith comes from hearing the message, and the message is heard through the word of Christ" (Rom. 10:17). This is not only true at the point of conversion; it is true throughout. We are not to look "in here" to find faith but to "fix our eyes on Jesus, the Pioneer and Perfecter of our faith" (Heb. 12:2).

In the Bible view, faith is a response to God's revelation of himself.

It is not based on man's own discovery of some new knowledge. It is not based on philosophical speculation as to what might possibly be. Rather, God has made himself known to us in history through the things he has said and the mighty deeds he has done. The revelation of God is the basis upon which Christian faith is established. The Christian does not believe the unbelievable, but trusts in a God who has acted and spoken and made those actions and those words understandable to mankind.

Paul contrasted faith with sight in saying that the believer is to walk by faith and not by sight (2 Cor. 5:7). He was saying that faith is spiritual sight. Just as we use our eyes to see what is around us, we use faith to "see" what cannot be seen in the spiritual realm. In insisting that we are to live by faith and not by sight, Paul was declaring that the Christian will not be operating on the basis of the apparent reality of circumstances. He will rather be making his decisions and ordering his life on the basis of the unseen realities of God, which he understands from his Word.

If we are to live by faith and not by sight, we must check our faith in something of the same way that we check our sight. When you go to a doctor of optometry for a check of your eyesight, does he ask you to remove your eyeball so that he can examine it? No, he asks you to read a chart on the wall. He checks your sight by asking you to see. Checking our faith is the same. My faith is not so much dependent upon my ability to believe as it is upon my perception of the object of that faith. The object of my faith is God and his promises in his Word. Living by faith does not depend on how strong the God is whom I am believing. I have faith not in my faith, but in him.

A Faith That Knows Something

Faith has its focus outside of us. It is not some inward personal experience or some quality or virtue within us. It is a looking away to trust the God who is faithful. This focus of faith outside of us is typical of Hebrew thought. The Bible is not so much interested in man's feelings about God. Rather, man is urged to accept the fact of God and to trust him. This is faith. The attitude of the person is not analyzed. The emphasis is, rather, upon the worthiness of the God who can be trusted.

The strength or weakness of our faith is directly related to the accuracy of our knowledge and understanding concerning the nature and purpose of God. Our faith depends on knowing something factual about God. No man can come to God in salvation apart from the gospel message. He must hear to believe. Faith, then, is not reaching out to the unknown, unbelievable, unseen possibilities beyond our own understanding. Faith is rather, in the biblical view, a response on our part to a clear word from God.

Jesus promised that the Holy Spirit would guide us into all truth (John 16:13). This is especially important since knowing who God is and what he plans to do is the beginning point of faith. The Holy Spirit makes God's word of revelation come alive with hope in our hearts. This expectancy is the way God gives us faith by the work of the Holy Spirit and the word of revelation (Eph. 1:17 ff.). This hope is a personal expectancy that God will indeed fulfill what he has promised to do. Like a tender plant, this beginning of faith springs up in the parched ground of doubt. Like a ray of light penetrating the deep darkness of despair, this hope enlightens the heart of the seeker.

A man may go through life wishing to be a better person, a better husband, a better parent. He may wish for the ability to overcome the immorality in his life, to gain release from the guilt of sin which plagues him from the past. But this wishing is like a vapor of smoke in the air. The first wind of circumstance blows it away. It has no substance or foundation under it. Then he hears the promise "Belive in the Lord Jesus, and you will be saved" (Acts 16:31). The Holy Spirit causes this word of promise to be real to him personally. He responds within his own heart with hope.

Apart from the ministry of the Spirit man would never believe. It is God who gives faith. Paul wrote, "For it is by grace you have been saved, through faith—and this not from yourselves, it is the gift of God" (Eph. 2:8). Through his Word and by his Spirit God gives the very faith by which a man trusts him. As we have already said, it is not natural to man to turn away from himself and trust God. He must be divinely enabled. But when, through the word of the gospel, the Holy Spirit ignites that divine spark of faith in his heart, the choice is left to the individual whether to place his trust and confidence in God.

A Faith That Shows Itself

The Bible makes clear that our response of faith to God's revelation must take some practical form. It is true that God moves toward us first. It is his initiative. But there must be some movement on our side, on the human side. This movement of ours toward God is what is meant by faith. James wrote that faith without action is dead, nothing more than agreeing to some doctrines, not the living trust by which a person is saved (Jas. 2:17-26).

Jesus often told those he healed to do something specific to show their confidence in him. He told one to go and wash in the pool of Siloam (John 9:7), another to go and show himself to the priest (Matt. 8:4). He told one to pick up his bed and walk (Mark 2:11), another to stretch out his crippled hand (Matt. 12:13). There were others he told to confess their faith aloud (Matt. 9:28). All of these actions are expressions of faith. A faith that is never expressed is not a saving faith.

Baptism has important significance for conversion at this very point. Baptism is one's public demonstration, his outward confession of his faith in Jesus Christ. Baptism is the drama of death, burial, and resurrection by which the believer publicly declares his identification with Christ. Just as Jesus has died, so has the new convert died to the old way of life. Just as Jesus was raised from the dead by the power of God, so has the new believer been given new life by God's saving power.

Baptism has no saving power in itself. The power that saves rests with God alone. Nevertheless, real faith in God, in response to the word of the gospel and the conviction of the Holy Spirit, will lead a person to desire to be baptized in order to publicly express his confession of Christ. The Ethopian eunuch asked of Philip, after hearing of the atoning death of Christ, "Look, here is water. Why shouldn't I be baptized?" (Acts 8:36). He wanted to release the faith that welled up within his heart by publicly demonstrating before Philip and all of the accompanying entourage that he was identifying with Jesus Christ as the one who alone paid the price for his sin.

With the advent in modern revivalism of the public invitation has come a somewhat different pattern of confession. Instead of calling upon one to "repent and be baptized" (Acts 2:38), the invitation is to "walk the aisle" to publicly confess one's faith in Christ. In most evangelical churches where an invitation is given, the response to the invitation itself becomes the high point of public confession. The congregation is asked to come by and greet the new believer to express thir joy and pledge their prayers. Baptism seems at times to be anticlimactic. Some churches have the baptism on the same day. Others delay the baptism until some training is given in the Christian faith.

Faith must be expressed outwardly if it is to follow the New Testament pattern of confession. A faith that lies dormant in the heart is not a faith that saves. It may be a good intention. It may be a confidence in the truth of the gospel. It may be a kindly feeling toward Jesus. It may even be a concern for one's own relationship with God. But faith does not issue in the beginning of a transformed life until that faith shows itself outwardly.

Inward and Outward Faith

The inner trust and outer confession of faith are clear in what Paul wrote in Romas 10:9-10: "If you confess with your mouth, 'Jesus is Lord,' and believe in your heart that God raised him from the dead, you will be saved. For it is with your heart that you belive and are justified, and it is with your mouth that you confess and you are saved." Here we see stated twice the twofold pattern of inward and outward confession. Both are necessary for conversion.

In the New Testament the resurrection is the key event which proved the lordship of Jesus. He had paid the price; salvation was bought; and he rose to life anew. So when we believe in our hearts that he is raised from the dead and confess with our mouth that he is Lord, we express confidence in the full scope of the atonement of Christ.

A survey taken in the counseling rooms of a major evangelistic enterprise questioned those who came for assurance of their salvation. The survey revealed that some 80 percent of those who were unsure of their salvation indicated that they did not pray aloud at the time of their conversion. Why should it be that a person who prayed silently in his surrender to God would be unsure of his salvation at a later time? Could it be that Paul gave us the answer in Romans 10? "If you confess with your mouth, 'Jesus is Lord,' " he wrote. When a person confesses with his mouth, he shows he actually has believed in his heart.

Psychologists tell us that we really do not know what we think until we get our thoughts out into verbal words. There is a psychological principle involved here, but there is a spiritual principle as well. There is a dynamic force about verbalizing what we really think and feel that makes this confession necessary to genuine faith. Framing faith in words and hearing the sound of your own voice in expressing it crystallizes and clarifies that faith.

We can never be sure what an inquirer is asking God to do in a counseling situation until we hear him pray aloud. Some are reluctant to pray aloud, preferring to pray in their hearts because they are not sure how to pray. But should we have an inquirer who doesn't know how to pray in the first place trying to pray silently? Even praying aloud is difficult when a person is not accustomed to prayer. But praying silently is all the more difficult. After a period of allowing random thoughts to run through his mind, an inquirer may be yet unsure what he has said in a silent prayer. As we call men to faith, let's not be reluctant to insist on an outward confession which will validate their inner trust.

It is clear, then, that the biblical concept of faith is dramatically different from the idea held by modern man. Biblical faith is indeed a faith that looks before it leaps. It is not a part of the nonrational and nonlogical. Biblical faith makes sense. It requires evidence. It begins with God and his Word. It is a reasonable faith directly related to our understanding of who God is and how he operates. Since biblical faith is tied to factual information, we can see how the factual gospel of Christ evokes valid saving faith.

Faith, in the biblical view, is not an experience. It is not a mysterious virtue within man. It is rather a divinely kindled confidence in the truth of God's revelation. It is God who gives faith. But this God-given faith must be deliberately exercised by man, or it is of no effect. It must be outwardly expressed to be inwardly effective. In calling men to Christ we call on them to believe. Our method is to simply declare the truth of Jesus' death for our sins and resurrection to victory. As God gives faith by his Spirit, men can then have "the righteousness that comes by faith" (Rom. 4:13).

One of the most certain truths concerning faith in the Bible is the assurance that God will respond. Faith is our response to God's revelation of his promises, which in turn brings a counter response in God. Again and again the Bible declares that God will act in response to our faith and confidence in him. Solomon said that not one word of all the promises of God had failed (1 Kings 8:56). Jesus made it clear that we need but ask, and God will act in response (Matt. 7:7-11,18,19; John 16:24). He promised that God will answer his children quickly (Luke 18:8).

This confidence of God's response is a great assurance to us in bringing the good news to a tangled world. The atonement of Christ is a historically completed eternal fact. Salvation is already accomplished. Forgiveness of sins for the whole world is already a reality (1 John 2:2). This is the good news we bear. All man has to do is believe. He is but to trust God by exercising the faith that is his at the hearing of the gospel. This and this only brings the reality of the atonement of Christ to bear in his personal relationship with God.

6
The Moving Parts of Conversion

I've always been fascinated with how things work. From the time I had my first set of Tinker Toys and Erector Set, my driving force was to build something with complex cranks, pulleys, and gears that actually worked. From there I moved to radio kits, miniature broadcast stations, and recording equipment. Perhaps you identify with that. Maybe you remember, too, taking those old watches and clocks apart just to see what made them tick.

An even more fascinating study is what makes a man tick. The workings of our inner selves pose a constant challenge to psychologists and psychiatrists. Only in recent decades has psychology been generally recognized as a science. Some are yet not sure that the complex unseen factors of our own personalities can be studied in a genuinely scientific way.

Our concern with bringing the good news of Christ to a tangled world necessarily narrows to the personal response of individuals to the gospel. Even mass evangelism must deal with the need for personal decision. Recent years have seen an increased concern among evangelistic counseling. Almost every evangelistic enterprise has its version of a simple gospel booklet, designed to make the task of the personal worker easier and more effective. Other training and materials are constantly being developed for help with assurance of salvation and growth in discipleship.

Yet the fact remains that those Christian groups so intensely interested in conversion are the ones most unsure about when a person is actually converted. Denominations which employ catechism schools and confirmation do not struggle with the question of conversion.

Groups holding to an educative approach to becoming a Christian do not fret over who is and who is not really saved. Rather, it is the evangelicals who seek to bring men to Christ through conversion who are so often concerned about whether a person has had a valid or authentic conversion experience.

What is conversion? What psychological factors are involved in it? Is there any way to be sure about one's conversion? How can we recognize an authentic conversion in the counseling situation? How much knowledge is necessary for conversion? How much emotional response is necessary? What is actually involved in the decision to believe in Jesus Christ? How much moral conviction is necessary? What is the role of the counselor? What is the role of the Holy Spirit?

These questions and many more we could raise all focus attention on the point in evangelism where "the water hits the wheel." Our entire purpose in evangelism narrows ultimately to the personal response of the individual to the gospel. In this chapter we will offer a biblical interpretation of the psychology of conversion. We will first consider the nature of biblical psychology. Then we will summarize key principles involved in a biblical view of man's psychology. Finally, we will attempt to apply these principles to the matter of conversion.

Understanding Biblical Psychology

The Bible explains man in a distinctive view which can be contrasted with other modern viewpoints. The position of materialism is that man is only what he eats and that his thinking is but a device provided by nature to help him in his real business of getting food. Rationalism says, on the other hand, that man is primarily what he thinks, that his doing is just something that comes from his reasoning. The Bible, though, affirms the reality of body and mind and does not concentrate on one or the other as the most important. The biblical view focuses on man's heart as the center of his being.

Biblical psychology is marked by several significant characteristics. It is theologically oriented, always seeing man in terms of his relation to God. It is practical, being more interested in describing what a man says or does than in analyzing why. Its terminology is flexible and nontechnical, with a good bit of overlapping in the meaning of various psychological terms. Biblical psychology is simple, seeing man as a creature of earth with the breath of God in him. It is functional, describing man as a whole in terms of various normal abilities and activities characteristic of him. It is nonsystematic, making no organized attempt to set forth a psychological description of man.

Any terminology used to describe aspects of psychological activity is figurative at best. The words in the Bible that are translated *heart, mind, soul, spirit, will,* and *conscience* represent ideas about the characteristics and capacities of man. They are not intended to describe psychological organs or faculties. These words reflect a vocabulary which came into use in an effort to explain the different ways a person can function in addition to purely physical activity. As we have noted, those who wrote the Scriptures never intended to present a systematic psychology. Nevertheless, in what they did write we can see a distinctive understanding of man in his psychological aspects.

A simple explanation of the biblical view of psychology is not possible, even after an extensive study of the various terms used. Space here will not allow a careful examination of the biblical words for heart, soul, conscience, and so forth. It will be more practical to share some of the key insights that have come from such a study. We will attempt to relate each truth to the challenge of evangelism for an understanding of the moving parts of conversion.

A Creature of God

The most important factor in the biblical view of man is his relationship to God. In contrast to modern views of man, the Bible sees his only claim to importance in his relationship with God. Our analysis of biblical psychology must, therefore, be done with this fact in mind. We must interpret man's psychological capacities and limitations in light of God's redemptive purpose. In the biblical view a person's capabilities for reasoning, thinking, responding emotionally, or making decisions are all seen in light of his basic need for being reconciled with God.

Psychology in the Bible is actually but an incidental area touched on occasionally as the main subject matter is pursued. The purpose of the biblical writers was not to identify and catalog psychological phenomena. Rather, they wrote from the viewpoint of faith in an effort to describe the redemptive action of God in history. Their purpose was to describe man as a sinner desperately in need of the salvation that could come only at the hands of a mighty God. Any psychological references were made as parts of this discussion.

We must never be lulled into a complacency about the basic need of man by his apparent ability to cope with his psychological difficulties. Symptoms of psychological stress are some of the most common evidences of man's estrangement from God. He may be guilt-ridden, frustrated, depressed, and confused. Through various forms of psychotherapy, some are able to deal with these problems and dull the pain of psychological distress. But apart from a right relationship with God, these "cures" may be short-lived. The symptoms may reappear in some other form. We must never lose sight of the fact that modern man is still fallen man and still desperately in need of the transformation that comes only by the power of God.

A Corrupted Nature

The corruption of man's nature because of his estrangement from God in sin affects every aspect of his psychological makeup. His mind is blinded in unbelief (2 Cor. 4:4), hostile toward God, and not subject to his law or able to be so (Rom. 8:7). His appetites are those of the "flesh," the fallen nature which stands in opposition to the Spirit of God (Gal. 5:16-17). He is enslaved to sin, and the members of his body are instruments of unrighteousness (Rom. 6:13).

In the biblical view the heart is the psychological term for the central and unifying element of personal life. Everything that determines the character of a person—his thoughts, plans, attitudes, fears and hopes—all lie in the recesses of his heart. The Bible description of the heart is consistent throughout. The heart of man in general is corrupt (Jer. 17:9), undependable (Prov. 28:26), and full of evil (Gen. 8:21; Eccl. 9:3). His heart issues in evil thoughts, murder, adultery, sexual immorality, theft, false testimony, and slander (Matt. 15:19).

It is only from this corrupted nature that the normal responses of man arise. He cannot by his own strength be other than what he is—a sinner alienated from God, fallen and corrupt at the very core of his being. His outlook on life, his moral values, his spiritual perception, his intellectual slant, and his emotional responses are all characteristic of his nature as fallen man. We are never surprised at the dogness characteristic of a dog. Neither should we be surprised at the kind of things which are characteristic of fallen man.

Measles cannot be cured by putting antiseptic on the spots because there is a virus in the bloodstream which must be eliminated. So is sin so pervasive a force that touches man from the core of his being to the edges. We must make clear that attempts at being better do not solve the problem of sin. They may but delay the only effective cure. Sin at the root of man's nature is not merely a problem of poor attitudes or bad behavior. It is a problem of alienation from God and the enthronement of self. Man is not only a sinner by nature but a sinner by choice as well.

Change Needed Within

The moral and spiritual responses of man must be changed, reformed, and redirected from within by the power of God from without. We have already noted that the attitudes, speech, and behavior of man comes from his nature. An attempt to change that inner nature by changes in outward actions will never work. It is a basic principle of biblical truth that nature determines behavior. Behavior does not determine nature. A dog does not become a dog by acting like one; he acts like a dog because he is one. In the same way every facet of man's life stems from his nature. Changes in who he is and what he does will come only with a basic change within.

The only answer for the condition of fallen man is provided in the atonement of Christ. A dramatic and fundamental change is required in man. "Make a tree good and its fruit will be good . . . " Jesus said, "for a tree is recognized by its fruit" (Matt. 12:33). Unless man is born again, he explained, he cannot see the kingdom of God (John 3:3). This radical change can become a reality. This redemptive transformation is not some devotional or mystical matter that affects a person only at a surface level. It issues in a new identity at the core of his being.

An important theme in the Bible concerning the heart is that it can be transformed by God's grace. Man is unable to overcome the leaning of his heart toward evil or to educate it sufficiently to be good. His only hope is a divine act of change that God accomplishes in his heart. God will create a new heart in the penitent sinner (Ps. 51:10). One day he will take away the old hardened heart of Israel and put a new, receptive heart in its place (Ezek. 36:26).

God has shone into the heart of the believer to give him the light of the knowledge of the gospel (2 Cor. 4:6). It is there that Christ himself can dwell (Eph. 3:17) and his peace reign (Col. 3:15).

The Christian has a new nature (2 Cor. 5:17) as a son of God (Rom. 8:15). He has new psychological capabilities: a new discernment of good and evil (Heb. 5:14); a new sensitivity to the needs of others (1 John 3:14); a new ability for sound judgment (2 Tim. 1:7); a cleansed conscience (Heb. 10:22); a new power for decision, which comes of being freed from sin's power (Rom. 6:6-7); a new ability by God's grace to choose the will of God unto righteousness (Rom. 6:12-14). The believer thus realizes a new identity as a man in Christ.

Some modern writers believe that the nature of man is changing for the better. We are told by the semisciences such as parapsychology that man has only begun to tap the vast resources of his own intellectual, emotional, and psychic capacities. New methods of finding inner peace such as Transcendental Meditation promise serenity and well-being plus a host of other benefits. We must not forget, though, that any approach to improving man that does not deal with the basic problem of sin is doomed to disappointment. These remedies are like putting a Band-aid on a broken leg. Man suffers a fragmentation of his being at the deepest level, and only the power of God can bring healing.

Focusing Beyond the Self

The Bible presents an objective moral and spiritual focus rather than a subjective one. The focus is outside the individual on the objective reality of God and his purpose. The emphasis is not upon man and his inner feelings and impressions. The biblical concepts of mind, soul, conscience, and faith are all seen as dependent upon the reality of facts outside the person for the determination of their effectiveness. How these psychological capacities are related to God is a matter of first importance in the Scriptures. So the inner feelings of man are considered to be relatively unimportant. The reality of God is the emphasis.

A man's values, his priorities, his loyalties are the factors that determine his character. He reflects whatever object of his concern he considers to be most worthwhile. He is warned to weigh his priorities carefully, for where a man's treasure is there will his heart (basic character) be (Matt. 6:21). The character of the soul is determined and defined in terms of the object toward which a person moves or makes his decisions. In Jesus' parable of the rich fool (Luke 12: 16-21) the man says, "Soul, you have many goods laid up for many years to come; take your ease, eat, drink and be merry" (v. 19, NASB). It is obvious in this story that the decision of the soul sets the direction and determines the value of that soul with reference to God's purpose.

The absence of a developed idea of conscience in the Old Testament is probably due to the conviction that the fear of the Lord, rather than the knowledge of self, is the beginning of wisdom (Prov. 1:7; 9:10). The New Testament understanding of conscience is rooted in this Old Testament idea. In the Hebrew way of thinking, authority for faith and conduct does not come from within a person. Moral action and character are measured by the external revelation from God rather than by the inner standards of a man's own thinking. So the point of reference for conscience in the Bible is objective—that is, outside of a man, rather than subjective, within a man.

The biblical emphasis on the reality outside of man as his point of reference has much to say to us in the task of evangelism. There is a trend today toward the idea that one person's idea is as good as another's, that there is no real objective truth, that experience should be dominant over any so-called "truth." This outlook is just the opposite of the biblical view. We do not ask a man how he feels about God; we rather tell him what God thinks about him. We do not ask him to search within to find God; we point him beyond himself to the holy Creator who stands above creation. We do not ask modern man to speculate as to what might be necessary to be right with God; we rather tell him that God has made his will clearly known in Christ. We do not ask man to attempt a rehabilitation program for human nature; we point him to the mighty salvation of God already accomplished in his behalf.

Freedom Only in Surrender

We usually think of *free will* as meaning that man has, at least within some limits, the power to choose his own path. He can submit to or reject motives that arise within him as well as influences from without. Therefore, he can modify his own character to some degree. But the idea of moral freedom found in the Scriptures is different from this. From the biblical viewpoint, real freedom is having the power to act according to God's purpose. Anything that limits a person's power to fulfill God's intention for him is a bondage of some sort.

A basic concept in New Testament thinking is that a man chooses his own master and becomes a slave to that choice. Paul writes that when a man presented himself to some authority for obedience, he was the slave of that one he obeyed. The two choices he named are "sin which leads to death, or to obedience, which leads to righteousness" (Rom. 6:16). God sets the believer free to serve himself. The only other master is sin. Jesus said that "everyone who sins is a slave to sin" (John 8:34). Man chooses what appears to be release from the demands of righteousness, but finds himself bound in the chains of his own counterfeit freedom.

In the biblical view man is free to choose but not free from the necessity of choosing. He is free to choose his master but not free from the rule of that master. He is free to make decisions at every point where they are called for but not free from the consequences of the decisions he makes. In short, whether he likes it or not, man must choose on God's terms. Freedom was thrust upon him by God. Neither the freedom nor the necessity of it was evil, but in both was the potential for evil. God created man with moral freedom and saw him exercise it disastrously in Adam's fall into sin. Nevertheless, God did not move the divine boundaries to that freedom or neutralize the results for it that came with the fall.

In bringing the good news of Christ to a tangled world, we can be assured of a man's freedom to respond in faith. But we must not be fooled by the humanistic belief in man's total freedom as master of his world. The freedom we enjoy is limited at several important points. It is limited by man's fallen nature in sin. Though he is free to exercise his will and choose as he sees fit, man will choose as befits his fallen nature. His freedom is limited further by his own understanding. Since he is limited to purely human perception (1 Cor. 2:4-5), his insight into any decision is severely restricted. Man is limited also in his ability to carry his decisions into action. He knows he should, but he cannot do the right things he decides to do (Rom. 8:18).

The decision making involved in conversion is a spiritual transaction. A person cannot be converted anytime he may choose. This decision and the motivation for it are not natural to man. He must be divinely enabled. God works to draw a person to Christ (John 6:44), shine into his heart with understanding (2 Cor. 4:6), convict him of sin (John 16:8), grant him repentance (Acts 11:18), and give him faith (Eph. 2:8). Our confidence of response as we present the gospel does not lie with our assurance of man's interest and willingness to be converted. Our confidence is in the faithfulness of God to draw men unto himself. The impulse and drive for conversion is with God, "who wants all men to be saved and to come to a knowledge of the truth" (1 Tim. 2:4).

Aiming for Action

Man's thinking and deciding are seen in the Scriptures as related to action. There is no room for thinking and decision making as mental exercises with no action in mind. Unless a person's intention to follow Christ is carried out in action, a decision is not really made. The emphasis on man's physical life also stresses the necessity for a harmony between intention and action. Man's faith response to the gospel of Christ must take place not only in his heart, but also outwardly in some visible fashion.

The necessity of an outward expression is at the very root of the nature of biblical faith. It is also fundamental to biblical concepts of thinking and decision making. The evangelical emphasis upon a public confession of faith is valid in the Scriptures and in fact vital to conversion. Secret disciples, reluctant converts, and professions of faith with reservations are nowhere condoned in the Scriptures. Jesus made his desires clear when he said, "Whoever acknowledges me before men, I will also acknowledge him before my Father in heaven. But whoever disowns me before men, I will disown him before my Father in heaven" (Matt. 10:32-33).

Conscience: Moral Witness Within

A most important psychological concept for our study is the idea of conscience. The concept of conscience in the New Testament is closely tied with the word *sumeidesis.* This word is a combination of *sum,* which means together with, and *eidenai,* which means to know. So the basic meaning of the New Testament word for conscience is "knowing together with yourself." Conscience is actually the power within a person of moral testimony. It is a witness felt and known within that warns a man about the rightness or wrongness of some past behavior or some he is planning. But conscience does not lay down moral standards itself. It works with whatever knowledge and convictions a person has.

We discover fairly quickly from New Testament passages that conscience is not a perfect guide. Paul wrote of a weak conscience which is unable to speak with authority (1 Cor. 8:10-12). Conscience may also be "evil" or "defiled" through knowing that wrong choices are being made (Heb. 10:22; Titus 1:15). Paul also wrote of those who have their consciences "seared as with a hot iron" (1 Tim. 4:2), hypocritical liars who teach the deceptive doctrines of demons. On the other hand, conscience may be "pure" or "unveiled" (2 Tim. 1:3), giving an honest and clear moral testimony. Conscience may be "clear" or "honorable" as a person tries to live honestly in every respect (Acts 24:16; Heb. 13:18).

Conscience is actually more effective in revealing the character of a person than the moral quality of his behavior. In other words, the voice of your conscience tells more about you than it does about the particular moral issue in question. For this reason conscience cannot by itself justify a man in the sight of God. Paul wrote that he was conscious of nothing against himself, and yet realized that he was not justified before God by this. He said that the one who would examine his life was the Lord himself (1 Cor. 4:4). The fact that every man looks at right and wrong through the color of his own character makes it clear that a person's good feeling about himself is not sufficient for acceptability with God.

The effectiveness of conscience is determined to a large degree by the spiritual condition of a person's heart. Every man is in need of a reconciliation with God (2 Cor. 5:20). Only by this reconciliation can the conscience come to a joyous sense of forgiveness and free access to God. The Bible offers no cleansing agent for the conscience of man other than the blood of Christ, which alone gives acceptability before God (Heb. 9:14). Therefore, only the believer can have a pure, clear, and clean conscience by biblical moral standards. We only experience a disposition of moral joy as we continue in an attitude of faith, trusting the adequacy of the atonement of Christ for our sins.

It is the conscience to which the law of God appeals in a person. Unless one is confronted with the law, he will not realize that his sin is not only a personal distress and social problem but a source of estrangement with God. Paul indicated that one purpose of the law is to lead us to Christ (Gal. 3:24). As one hears the moral "oughts" of the Scriptures his conscience is disturbed at his standing before God. The conviction of the Holy Spirit unites with the awakened conscience to produce a godly sorrow, which brings repentance that leads to salvation (2 Cor. 7:8-11). Especially in our day of relative values, man needs to hear of God's absolute standards of righteousness. Only then does he cry out, "God, have mercy on me, a sinner" (Luke 18:13).

Defining Conversion

The word translated *conversion (epistrophe)* appears only once in the New Testament (Acts 15:3). The verb "to be converted" *(epistrepho)* appears only six times. Another form of the word meaning nearly the same thing *(strepho)* appears one time. The meaning of the word *(epistrepho)* is quite simple, to turn about or to turn upon. It means to make a radical change, one that will result in a significant difference in direction, orientation, values, and loyalties. The word *conversion* is used in modern language with the meaning of a change or transformation. Even though the word is not used often in the Scriptures, the idea is still prominent; and conversion still best describes the initial response to the gospel that evangelism seeks.

The psychological insights that we have identified from the Scriptures offer further understanding of the meaning of conversion. Since man's relationship to God is primary in the Bible, conversion is of great importance. Man's fallen nature shows itself in everything he does. Only a basic change at the core of his being can correct this problem. But the resources for that change are not within man. Conversion comes only as a person looks beyond himself to God and turns to trust him for salvation. Since man's corrupted nature makes conversion an unnatural choice, he must be divinely enabled to see the spiritual nature of the decision and follow through on it. Since the Bible sees decision as necessarily issuing in action, conversion must involve an outward expression. The pangs of conscience are not alone the conviction needed for repentance. But through one's realization of sin and the conviction of the Spirit, conscience plays a major role in conversion.

Conversion, then, comes with that initial response of faith by which a person accepts the reality and power of Christ's atonement for his sin. He is, therefore, justified by faith. The Holy Spirit gives spiritual life, and the new Christian has a new nature because of the Spirit's indwelling presence. Every aspect of his selfhood is affected as his new center of focus is in Christ and not self. His outlook, his moral sensitivity, his discernment of spiritual values, and his appetite for the things of God all reveal a dramatic change in the new convert. He has a new sense of peace and a confidence of acceptability with God. These changes are not merely a matter of devotional self-control or expectation based on the power of religious suggestion. This fundamental change is an actual transformation at the center of a person's being.

We began this chapter talking about the moving parts of conversion. The Bible, though, does not see man psychologically in terms of parts. Soul, mind, heart, and will are not parts but ways of describing a person from different points of view. Nevertheless, we can identify various psychological functions of man that are involved in conversion. There is the intellectual aspect of man's capabilities—his knowing, reasoning, and understanding. There is also the moral sensitivity of man, which makes its witness heard as conscience both in the mind and the emotions. Then there is the volitional capacity of man—his ability to choose and decide. A fourth psychological function is the emotional, which has to do with his feelings and desires. We will examine these four basic functions as the moving parts of conversion.

The Necessary Knowledge

How much knowledge is necessary for conversion? It is obvious as we consider man in his intellectual capacity that a certain amount of knowledge and understanding will be involved in any decision he makes. We will have to affirm, then, that a certain amount of knowledge is necessary for conversion. Paul wrote that "faith comes from hearing the message, and the message is heard through the word of Christ" (Rom. 10:17). He was here raising the issue of knowledge for conversion. He asked, "How, then, can they call on one of whom they have not heard? And how can they hear without someone preaching to them?" (Rom. 10:14). Conversion faith will require knowing something.

The gospel itself is content oriented. It is a message we are sharing. We are not primarily sharing an experience. We are not sharing a religion. We are not sharing a ritual exercise. We are not sharing a new set of moral laws. The very thrust of evangelism is that we are sharing a message—that content of information about the life, death, burial, and resurrection of Jesus Christ as he made atonement for our sins. Paul was confident of this message. He wrote, "I am not ashamed of the gospel, because it is the power of God for the salvation of everyone who believes: first for the Jew, then for the Gentile. For in the gospel a righteousness from God is revealed, a righteous that is by faith from first to last, just as it is written: 'The righteous will live by faith' " (Rom. 1:16-17).

Let's notice where this knowledge is focused. It is not self-knowledge, but knowledge of an event outside oneself. Any self-understanding associated with conversion is a reflective response to the knowledge of the atonement of Christ. We must avoid the trap of emphasizing self-knowledge as a key to conversion. The basic knowledge needed is the simple message of the gospel: Jesus Christ died for your sin—*Jesus,* the historically revealed Son of God. He is *Christ,* the anointed Messiah of Israel. He *died* as an atoning sacrifice to remove the barrier between man and God. It was as a substitute *for* man that he died, was risen, and intercedes today at the throne of God. It was on *your* behalf that Jesus died, as though you personally and individually were the only one in need of salvation. It was for *sin,* that self-exalting, God-rejecting force that has man in its power. Though as much information as is appropriate should be given, these basic truths are the core of the gospel message.

We must make clear that intellectual information alone is not adequate for conversion knowledge. A person must have an understanding of the significance of that knowledge that comes only through the enlightenment of the Holy Spirit. The role of the Christian witness is to present the message. He does not have the power to elicit an understanding of that message or a spiritual response of faith to it. He presents the gospel of Christ in full dependence upon the ministry of the Spirit. He must leave the enlightening and convicting work in the hands of God. This does not relieve him, though, of the responsibility of giving as clear and persuasive a witness as is possible to him.

The Moral Issue

Inherent in the gospel message is the concept of sin. It was for sin that Jesus died that man might be restored to fellowship with God. As we have said, sin is not merely a matter of personal failure and social embarrassment; it is an offense against God. Jesus did not die primarily to give man the ability to overcome his failure. He did not die to ease his embarrassment before his fellowman. Jesus died to overcome the estrangement that sin brings between man and God. It is the law of God, the "ought" of the Scriptures, which spells out man's offense against a holy and righteous Creator. It is man's conscience that corresponds to the law. The law is not primarily rational, emotional, or volitional. It is moral. So it is moral conviction awakened by the law that produces a godly sorrow leading to repentance.

Conscience plays a key role in conversion. It represents man's moral sensitivity to the "ought" of God. Our basic evangelistic appeal, then, must be an appeal to conscience. It is not man's ignorance that separates him from God. It is not his emotional dullness. It is not his weak willpower. It is his moral failure. This moral failure is not only a matter of deeds, words, and thoughts recorded against him. His moral dilemma is as deep as the fallen human nature that has produced that bad record. If ignorance were man's problem, we might make an intellectual appeal to his rational and logical sense. If emotional insensitivity were the cause of man's estrangement from God, we might want to try stimulating his emotions. If volitional failure were his problem, we might appeal for willpower. But since the problem is sin, we must appeal to conscience for repentance.

We are dealing here with the question of motivation for conversion. Why is it a person comes to God for salvation? Is it because he feels sorry for the crucified Christ? Is it because he is afraid for himself? These may be part of the motivation at times. But the strongest impulse and that most true to the Scriptures is a sense of guilt, a conviction of sin. As we have already noted, the Holy Spirit is at work in the world to convince people of sin, of righteousness, and of judgment (John 16:8). If we are to cooperate with the Spirit in evangelism, we will want to present the truth that awakens a conviction of sin. Not until a person is convinced of his sin will he cry out for salvation from sin.

The Conversion Experience

How much emotion is necessary for conversion? There has been a good deal of discussion in evangelism concerning experience, emotion, some display of personal agony or joy. We have come to refer to a "conversion experience." But the Bible does not discuss conversion primarily in experiential terms, even though there is definitely an experiential aspect to conversion. We must avoid the trap of measuring the authenticity of conversion by the amount or kind of experience involved. Conversion does not depend for its validity on a certain kind of or intensity of experience.

I have heard evangelists say, "You must go back and examine your experience to determine whether you are really saved." This kind of statement seems to indicate that the quality, degree, intensity, or kind of experience a person has is the determining factor in conversion. The Bible does not indicate that this is the case. Rather than emphasizing the saving experience of man, it points to the saving experience of Jesus. We do not read in the Scriptures of a "faith experience." Faith is rather pictured as a trust in God beyond the ebb and flow of experience.

Let's identify experience in conversion as an emotional prelude and aftereffect of one's faith commitment. A person will respond experientially according to his temperament, his background, his own conception of his sin before God. His response is as unique and individual as the person himself. It has much to do with cultural and social circumstances. Certain groups tend to respond in like terms in conversion. Even though the conviction, release, and joy that are manifested may be important indicators of what is taking place, we must not imply that one person's salvation is of better quality than another's because he showed more emotion.

Though human experience is not our guarantee of the quality

of salvation, we can know something of a person's attitude and faith by the nature of his experience at conversion. An expression of genuine faith in the atonement of Christ is followed by a sense of release from the burden of sin, by a sense of joy and peace with God. One who apparently professes Christ but senses no release from the burden of guilt and no peace with God may be assumed to have reservations about the commitment. He may be attempting to please someone else by going through the motions of professing Christ. He may be yet unsure that complete provision has been made for his sins. He may be reserving to himself some degree of control over his own life. Our need on such occasions is to be sensitive to these possibilities and to try to counsel a person toward the truth.

Assurance is often attached to experience. As we have noted, though, an attempt to examine the quality of one's experience (perhaps of years ago) implies that salvation is dependent on that experience rather than upon the experience of Christ. Where was the salvation of God accomplished? Some preachers have urged Christians to "drive down a stake" by making a clear expression of commitment to Christ that can ever after serve as a guarantee of their salvation. We must understand, through, that the stake was driven down once and for all in the crucifixion of Christ. It was his experience and not ours God intended as the mighty work of his salvation. We are to "fix our eyes on Jesus, the Pioneer and Perfecter of our faith, who for the joy set before him endured the cross, scorning its shame, and sat down at the right hand of the throne of God" (Heb. 12:2).

Making a Decision

The fourth of the moving parts of conversion is the volitional function of man, his capacity for decision. Man may not see the goodness of the law of God and wish for it in his own life, but he is unable to decide to do that will and fulfill it in action (Rom. 7:14-25). His fallen nature corrupts all the powers necessary to decision. Only through an enabling by the Holy Spirit can man be given the choice involved in conversion. The Spirit enlightens his understanding of the gospel, convicts him of his need, exalts Christ as the risen Savior, and gives him the faith to believe for salvation. Even so, when actually facing the decision, he can accept or reject God's salvation as he chooses.

Any genuine decision must be expressed outwardly, or no decision is actually made. This is a psychological principle as well as a spiritual one. I remember trying to decide to jump off the swimming pool high-diving board when I was a boy. I struggled with the decision until people behind me on the ladder grew impatient. But the decision was never really made until I left the board. Several times before that I thought I had decided, but my failure to jump proved I had not. No matter how many times a person says "I will do it" in his heart, he is not converted until he openly cries out for salvation and outwardly expresses what he inwardly longs to do.

Though the outward expression of conversion faith might take any number of forms, it is best to begin with an audible prayer. We have already discussed the matter of a faith that shows itself (chapter 5). Therefore, we will not pursue the matter further here. Let me add, though, that the outward expression of conversion faith should be appropriate to the nature of salvation. Of course, baptism perfectly pictures the believer's identification with Christ in death, burial, and the resurrection to a new life. Even before a new convert is baptized, though, he should be urged to share his testimony of conversion with friends and family. It may be helpful for him to write it out. This also helps the pastor discern the new convert's comprehension of what has happened and how.

These, then, are the moving parts of conversion. We have noted that at several points biblical psychology is not in harmony with modern thinking. We have also noted that the gospel is of a distinctive nature and must be carefully honored if we are to be effective in evangelism. The ministry of the Holy Spirit is also of great importance. As we understand what the Spirit is doing and how he works, we can better share the gospel in such a way as to cooperate in his divine work. What a joy it is to know that God understands every man—even the deep mysteries of his life. What a joy to know that the gospel of Christ is adequate to meet every need, that the salvation of God is complete.

7
The Gospel in Plain Clothes

My daddy loved to tell a tale about the country boy who came home for Thanksgiving after one semester at the university. His somewhat untutored father wanted to show him off to the kinfolks gathered on the porch. "Son, tell us what you been studyin' at the university." Somewhat embarrassed, the boy replied, "Well, geometry for one thing." "Say some jomertry for us," the older man demanded, proudly looking around to see how impressed his uncles and cousins were. "Oh, Daddy, you don't talk geometry; you draw it." "You mean I spent all that money to send you up there to learn jomertry and you can't talk none of it?" the old man complained. "You talk me some jomertry right now before I lose my patience with you," he ordered. "Well, all right," the boy gave in. "Pi r square," he said. The father just looked at him. "Is that it?" he asked. "Yes, sir, " came the meek reply. "Pie are square. Pie are square," the old man repeated in disbelief. "Is that all they learned you up there? Any derned fool knows better'n that," he shouted. "Pie are not square. Pie are round. Cornbread are square!"

Effective communication is never easy. Sometimes it seems almost impossible. Many of us have experienced the problems created by the technical language of any field when these specialized words are used with laymen. I am always perturbed when anyone—a medical specialist or a building contractor, to name two—uses his trade language with me, a layman. Especially exasperating are the medical abbreviations and initials that are thrown around as though I'm supposed to know what they mean. Every specialized area of study considers the rest of the world laymen. We have used the term *layman* in Christian circles to classify everybody but the clergymen. But even our laymen tend to pick up what has been called the *language of Zion,* the specialized terminology of the Christian "in" group.

In bringing the good news of Christ to a tangled world our primary task is communication. We have already discussed the analogies and metaphors of the Scriptures, which help us explain the gospel truth to modern man. We are yet left, though, with the problem of getting our message across. A favorite seminary prof used to urge us to share the gospel in "people talk." Even so, many of us who have studied a little theology wind up using a few fourteen-letter words which "regular people" probably do not understand. But there is more to effective communication than a careful choice of words. As we have noted, our day is not like the first century. We must share the good news in a way our contemporaries can grasp.

Even with the use of people talk and a sensitivity to our modern way of life, we still face problems in communication. Ours is not a message we share indifferently. It is not of only casual importance. Ours is a life-and-death message with eternal consequences. When can we know our listener has actually *heard* our message? Is merely telling it enough? When have we actually communicated? How can we take the good news of Christ into the world and yet maintain our Christian distinctiveness? What about nonverbal communication, when ideas are conveyed without a word's being said? What is involved in communication besides words? The challenge of bringing the good news to a tangled world certainly merits a serious examination of the problem of communication.

When Have They Heard?

A common approach to communicating the gospel implies that the thought patterns of modern man are not different from those of the first-century man, to whom the New Testament was first addressed. Many witnesses are unaware of the basic principles of communication which must be honored in order for the message to be properly delivered. The usual approach puts the full emphasis on the telling of the message without much thought of the hearer. No attention is given to the unseen communication gap that must be bridged. Proclamation is equated with communication, telling with understanding.

Proclamation is only a part of communication. We actually have not communicated the message until it has been heard and understood. Further, we have not effectively communicated a message until it has been heard, understood, and accepted as a personally relevant bit of information. This last factor, acceptance, is especially important for the communication of the gospel of Christ. We may technically say that we have communicated, even though our message be heard, understood, but rejected. This is not to deny that our purpose is to have the message heard and understood and finally accepted.

The fact that the message is accepted does not mean that the person himself exercises saving faith in Christ. It merely means that the person sees that our message is a valid statement of truth. He sees that if he did act upon it, it would produce the results promised. Therefore, communication must involve a message which is proclaimed clearly, understood in the same meaning which was intended in the proclamation, and accepted as emotionally and intellectually valid in producing what it promises. This complete communication then leaves the hearer with a legitimate choice to make, whether to act upon the message or not.

Some most helpful insights in the communication of the gospel can be seen in Romans 10, beginning with verse 14. In this passage we read the following:

> How, then, can they call on the one they have not believed in? And how can they believe in the one of whom they have not heard? And how can they hear without someone preaching to them? And how can they preach unless they are sent? (Rom. 10:14-15).

The apostle Paul followed this passage by saying that not all the Israelites responded to the good news. Faith comes from hearing the message, and the message is heard through the words of Christ. Then he asked, "Did they not hear?" "Of course they did," he said. He asked further, "Did they not understand?" This was the problem: they were without understanding (v. 19). He equated their lack of understanding with the fact that they were disobedient and obstinate people (v. 21). In this passage are the same elements we have mentioned above: the message being preached, the message being understood with the same meaning that was intended, the message being accepted.

I must hear what you mean rather than only what you say for real communication to take place. Therefore, the thought patterns of today's man must be carefully evaluated. In order for me to get the meaning that is the same as the meaning you have in mind, you must communicate in words and examples familiar to me. These words and examples must have the same meaning for me that they do for you. Here is where we must take a close look at the words we use to see whether what they mean to us will be the same as what they mean to modern man. We must translate words that make up the "house language" for us Christians into the words of the "street language" of secular man. This communication does not have to use profane language, but it must use the common language of the people. It must carry meaning that can be understood without having to spend a lot of time defining our words. We should remember that the New Testament was written in *koine* Greek. This was the common language of the people, the street language. It was different from classical Greek, the language of the scholars and philosophers. If we are to communicate that eternal biblical message in today's world, we also will have to use the language of the people.

Another important test for effective communication is to check the *purpose* we have in mind for our message to accomplish. Do we intend to have our hearer know something, or understand something, or feel something, or appreciate something, or do some serious thinking? Do we intend, on the other hand, for the response to be action—a decision of faith to surrender to Jesus Christ? We could present the gospel in a way that could cause a person to think about its logic. We could communicate the gospel in a dramatic way for an emotional response. We could share the gospel in a way that would lend itself to knowledge and understanding. We could also communicate the gospel in a form which would bring a response of appreciation. But if our purpose is evangelistic, then we should try to communicate the message in a way designed to call for repentance, faith, and surrender. In doing this, we will often see serious thought, emotion, understanding, and appreciation.

Learning the Language

The communication gap isn't closed by simply picking up the slang of whatever group you are with. Country people may think you're mocking them if you try to imitate their speech. The response would probably be the same with any group. We may even find ourselves saying what we hear them say but at the wrong time. We may think we know what "git all my coons up the same tree" means. But if we try to talk like that when we are not really a part of that cultural group, we sound phony and artificial. It would be better to say what we want to say in simple, uncluttered language.

I went with a group of students to a hippy halfway house in the late sixties. Young people from all over, mostly runaways, were there trying to get out of the drug trap. We were there to talk, to listen, and to share Christ. The situation was very informal in the large two-story house. As several of us gathered in one of the bigger rooms our leader sat down cross-legged on the floor and began to talk to the kids. In the course of his conversation he began to use expressions like "We just came here to rap (he meant talk)" or "Cool, man!" I could have crawled under the rug. Coming from a fortyish, bald, middle-class preacher, that just didn't fit. I am sure the young people appreciated his intentions. But it was obvious that he was using terms not normal to him. The result produced was an awkward artificiality.

To really communicate we must learn to use the simple language common to all of us. There will always be special missionaries to subculture groups who will want to "learn the language." But most of us will be sharing the gospel with a variety of groups, mostly rather ordinary people. I want to be "all things to my people," but that doesn't mean I should pretend I am one of them when I am not. I will want to be sensitive to the sound of my message in their ears. What I say will not sound the same in the ears of first-graders as it will to adults. But I need not pretend to be a first-grader to talk to one. Neither is it necessary for me to use all the latest elementary school slang. The same principle of sensitivity to how I'm being heard applies in every case, no matter how ordinary or how strange.

Of course, as soon as I say we should never use slang, I have to back off a bit. There will be times when we may want to use some of the favorite slang of a group as an expression of affection, a way of identifying with them. But the key point I want to stress is that we should be real. There is no doubt that our message is the truth of God, the salvation of everyone who will believe. But that truth will not sound with the ring of truth if the messenger is not quite true himself. We cannot use our choice of words to gain acceptance. We will rather gain acceptance when we are real and our words come out of Christlike motives.

A trap we may fall into in communicating the gospel is the use of biblical words that do not communicate to today's man. If we talk about *redemption* and use that Bible word, someone may be thinking of green stamps while we're thinking of the atonement of Christ. The *Lamb of God* is clear to us, but may call to mind an angelic sheep to someone who has never heard that expression. We may also unconsciously use other religious terminology that is not familiar to most people. *Share with me your experience with God* may mean nothing to someone for whom God is not personal and real. As we make an effort to understand these biblical ideas, we can then explain their significance to people without the use of specialized terminology they are not ready to hear.

The keys to effective communication may well be alertness and sensitivity. But we must not become nervous and uncertain to the point of being reluctant to share a witness at all. The Holy Spirit will work to give our witness the wings of conviction right into the heart of the person who hears it. We can trust the Spirit to do that. We must trust him. But trusting the Spirit does not mean becoming careless about our presentation of the message. The gospel of Christ deserves the best treatment we can possibly give it. It is a life-and-death message. It should be delivered with care.

Listening for the Hurt

What is a person primarily interested in? We could talk about a lot of things that interest people, but I can guarantee you that a person is primarily interested in himself. Whether we like it or not, this is a fact of human nature. If you and I are to get the attention of people to the gospel of Christ, we must touch some point at which their self-interest can be stimulated. We must come to them at a point where they are already motivated and awaken a response in them for interest in the message we have to present.

I remember hearing the story about the farmer who sold a plow mule to his neighbor. After an unsuccessful attempt to get the mule to work for him, the neighbor came back and complained that the mule wasn't nearly as good as had been claimed. The farmer went with him to see what the problem was. There was the mule, dug in with determination not to move a step. The farmer picked up a large fence post. Swinging with all his might, he hit the mule on the side of the head. Immediately the startled mule perked up and began to pull at the plow rigging. "Yep, I believe he will work now," he said. "What you have to do is get his attention first."

Let's be realistic about it. Many of the people living around you and me who do not know Christ are definitely not interested in knowing him. They have their own lives to interest and excite them. They have their own hopes, dreams, and goals for life. At the same time they have their own frustrations and discouragements, problems, and tragedies. No matter how skillfully a person orders his life without Christ, he will have an emptiness only God can fill. He will have needs he senses that come from his need of Christ. It is at this point we can definitely get a person's attention.

If we believe that a person without Christ lives a fragmented and disoriented life, then we can expect certain manifestations of that condition. We can expect to find frustration, guilt, discouragement, a lack of purpose, personal conflicts, and discord. When we do find these things, we can also assume that they are present because Christ is not in control in the life. When Christ is not in control in that life, we can know it because the person has not trusted his life into the hands of God and yielded to his control. We can reason from the symptoms back to the cause.

I counseled with a fifteen-year-old girl from a children's home after an evangelistic movie showing. She was there not because she was an orphan but because her parents did not want her. The theater had been filled with young people, including the special busload from the children's home. An evangelistic appeal was made at the end of the movie. Since there were so many inquirers, I was attempting to counsel at once with several from the children's home. As we sat in a circle I began by talking with this particular girl. She was hard, obviously embittered through years of frustration and rejection. Nevertheless, she had come in the invitation; so I assumed that God was dealing with her.

I asked, "Why did you come forward?" She said, "I came because I am so lonely." I asked her why she was so lonely with all these friends who were there with her. She said she had no real friends because nobody really liked her. She said nobody had ever loved her. I asked why she thought nobody ever loved her. She said she didn't know. She just knew they didn't. I said, "Sometimes you feel like nobody really loves you because when you look down inside, you think no one would love a person like that. You think you're the kind of person nobody could love." At this point tears began to come up in her eyes. She said, "Now you've got me doing something I never do." "What's that?" I asked. She said, "Cry."

She was hard. She'd never cried or at least wouldn't admit to having cried. She never did anything emotional like that. She had hardened herself against the experience of being hurt. I said, "Let me tell you some good news. God loves you just like you are. In spite of the fact that nobody else would love a person like you are down inside, God still loves you; and he wants to make you the kind of person down inside that everybody could love. Do you realize that Jesus died to make that possible? Do you know that God will take all that you are, all that sin, and forgive you and make it right?" As we continued to talk, several of the young people, including this one, prayed to receive Christ.

I have often wondered what difference there might have been in that conversation had I begun immediately with the fact that "all have sinned and come short of the glory of God," that "the wages of sin is death," and so on through the "Roman road." I believe that God in his grace would have worked to make Christ real to that young lady. I am confident that by his Spirit he would have made the word come alive. Nevertheless, it seems to me that he gives us a little sense to cooperate better with the Spirit by touching the point where people are really hurting. Where are these felt needs? Where is a person struggling with hurt and pain in his own life?

Could it be that if we start where somebody hurts, we will do a better job of leading that person to his real need? That real need is to be reconciled with God. The young lady I counseled with was sure of her felt need—loneliness. "Nobody loves me," she said. She did not know that the beginning of a new life for her was not in being cured of her loneliness, but in being made right with God. The loneliness was just a particularly painful manifestation of the fact that she was cut off from the God who made her. She needed to see that he is also the God who loved her enough to send Jesus

Christ on the most lonely mission ever experienced by man, the cross.

The gospel has a word for people wherever they are hurting. There is always some good news we can give them that directly relates to their felt needs. There's plenty of bad news in the world. Alienation, loneliness, frustration, discouragement, broken relationships, homes falling apart, and bondage of all kinds—all of this is bad news. We have a word of good news for a person that touches him at the very point of his bad news. The good news of the gospel of Christ will touch any sense of need a person feels. It will fit like a glove.

The New Testament indicates that there are definite results in the life of a person who comes to Christ. He has peace, joy, patience, and so forth (Gal. 5:22). All of these manifestations, called the fruit of the Spirit, are the result of the control of the Spirit of Christ in his life. When a person, on the other hand, is seeking to control his own life with his focus around self, he experiences a different set of results. It is not illogical to assume that when these results which express the control of the carnal nature are obvious in a person's life, Christ is not in control. As we help a person see this cause-effect relationship, we can lead him from his hurts to his real need to the answer of God's grace in Christ.

Treating the Real Disease

When you go to a doctor, how does he conduct an examination? He punches about here and there where you might have a problem and asks you whether it hurts. You tell him what the symptoms are—a pain here, a numbness there, a twitch or a discomfort of some kind. The doctor is not nearly so much interested in dealing with the symptoms as he is with finding the cause and setting it straight. In the process of treating the cause he will bring relief to the symptoms that brought us to him in the first place. He searches back from the symptoms to the real need. We must never forget that our purpose is to get behind the symptoms of man's fragmented life to the real problem of alienation from God.

We must recognize that the good news that directly applies at the point of a person's hurt is the good news of some benefit that comes from reconciliation with God in Christ. This is a matching of effect with effect. The hurt that a person feels is not the hurt of alienation from God, but of some symptom that springs from his alienation from God. So the hope that we give may not be, in the beginning, the hope of reconciliation with God, but the hope that that painful manifestation from which he suffers may be healed. Therefore, we often get a person's attention by talking to him about how Jesus Christ can bring a change at the point where he is hurting. Then we tell him the truth of the gospel message, which he urgently needs to hear.

In being alert for symptoms that indicate a person's felt needs, we must not come to the place of trying to solve these problems apart from dealing with the real need. We must not begin to concentrate on psychological difficulties in people and neglect their need to be right with God. We must not concentrate on helping people cope with their psychological problems in their present state when they really need to be born again. This is not because we do not have a sympathy for them in their struggles. Rather, it is because we must move from where they are hurting to lead them to an understanding of their real need. We must never come to the place of helping people to be more comfortable in their lostness.

The gospel did not come from man but from God. It came from a need which God perceived, not one felt by man. Some today say, "Leave us happy pagans alone." As Christians we are sometimes taken aback by such an attitude. But we must not measure a man's need for salvation by the degree of his distress of anxiety or by his own felt needs. We must measure the man's need for salvation by the degree of his real need as God has spelled it out. Man is a sinner whether he feels like it or not. He is lost and condemned whether he feels like it or not. He is disoriented and alienated from the will of God whether he knows it and experiences it or not. Certainly we do not wait for men to come to us—distraught, frustrated, guilty, and lost. We go, at the command of Christ, and proclaim the judgment of God and the good news of salvation in Jesus Christ.

The reason men today so often do not sense their need for Christ is that they have not seen the reality of their lostness. We must preach the judgment of God and his righteous standards for man until each man cries out in his own heart, "God, have mercy on me a sinner." Then we come to him with the good news of the gospel of Jesus Christ: "Jesus Christ has died for your sins." When we present our message to man in terms that God loves him and is willing to overlook his sins, we do him an injustice and discredit the gospel. We must ever recognize that God cannot have any fellowship with sin. We must make it clear that man's need as a lost and doomed sinner may not be revealed in his felt and thought and known needs.

Thus, we must come to man not on the basis of his experience, good or bad, but on the basis of God's Word. We must not promise man a better experience but promise him what God promises him, a restored relationship of fellowship with God, a reconciliation with his Creator, forgiveness of his sins through the blood of Jesus Christ. Certainly we will want to spell out the Christian life with all its benefits; but we must make clear that these are the fruits of the gospel, the results of a person's believing and accepting the sacrifice of Jesus Christ in his behalf. We touch on the felt needs of man to get his attention to the real disease and lead him to the remedy in the atonement of Christ.

More Than Words

One of the key ideas which we find in the Scriptures is the concept of the church as the body of Christ in the world. Jesus has given us a distinct role in the world. He has said we are the light of the world, the salt of the earth (Matt. 5:13-14). We are called a chosen people, a royal priesthood, a holy nation, whom God has called out of darkness into his wonderful light (1 Pet. 2:9). This concept of the distinctiveness of the Christian in the world will affect our concept of communicating in evangelism. We must learn that we communicate not only through what we say but through who we are. A person can read in our life-style, in our mannerisms, in our facial expressions, in our gestures, in our appearance much more than we often think he can. He can tell whether we are genuine or not, whether we are identifying with him or not, and whether we are focused on ourselves or whether we are focused on others.

It is interesting to note that Jesus' focus for his ministry was always on others. He was attentive to the needs of other people. He seemed to look into their lives, ferret out their needs, and identify with them. His focus of attention and the direction of his interest and concern were always from within himself, and his resources were outward toward the other person. He did not see people as those whom he could use or those who could do anything for him. We must get away from the idea of looking at another person for what he might be able to do for us.

How many times have you been introduced to someone and found five minutes later that you could not remember his name? I've wondered why this is the case in my own experience. I've come to the conclusion that the reason most of us have trouble remembering names when we are introduced is that at the point of introduction we are concentrating on what that person is thinking of us. Rather than thinking of the person to whom we are being introduced, we are actually thinking of ourselves and wondering whether we are making a good impression. We are intent upon smiling and shaking hands, being well thought of and respected. While this procedure may have some value, it indicates that our concentration of interest and concern is with ourselves rather than with the person to whom we are talking and the needs he may have.

One of the things we see in Jesus is that he talked about things that affected the people to whom he was talking. He dealt with people where they really lived and talked to them about those matters about which they were most concerned, speaking to them in terms they could understand. In his own heart and mind he was focusing on their interest and their concern. This is not to say that Jesus did not consider the primary issue to be the will and purpose of God. I believe the New Testament reveals that Jesus' purpose was that the will of God be done in his life, that he fulfill the pattern and plan for which he was sent into the world. Nevertheless, the focus and flow of Jesus' concern and interest was outward from himself toward the needs of people around him.

We communicate not only on a verbal and conscious level but on a subliminal, nonverbal level. Nonverbal communication is a most important matter for us. People pick up nonverbal cues from us that we never are aware of—a simple gesture, the movement of a hand, a turn of the eye, a movement of the eyebrow, the set of the mouth, the tone of a word—the way we say things rather than what we say. All of this communicates much that we may not realize. It communicates genuineness and sincerity, or it communicates coldness, or it communicates genuine interest and concern for people.

There may be techniques and principles that we could learn for mastering nonverbal and subliminal communication. But is this consistent with the Christian call for honesty? Let us rather learn to concentrate on the need, interest, and concern of the person to whom we are talking. Let's learn to look at him as a unique individual, celebrate his uniqueness, and thank God for him. Here is a person whom God made in his own image. Here is a person for whom Jesus died. Here is a person for whom God's love is flowing, a person to whom God has sent me for this appointment at this hour for sharing the good news of the gospel.

I have wondered why dogs and children respond to some people and not to others. I'm not sure that there is not some connection with the nonverbal, subliminal cues that are involved in this kind of communication. Could it be that dogs and children know people who are sincere, genuine, transparent, people who are not trying to make an impression? Better than we adults, they recognize people who are in themselves settled enough on who they are that they don't have to try to impress others. A part of our communication is actually who we are. If we can come to understand who we are in Christ and what has been made possible through the atonement, the identity we have in Christ, and the significance of the gospel message for bringing that same identity to others, we can begin to communicate with those who do not know Christ.

Incarnational Evangelism

We might call this communication of the gospel with words and more than words "incarnational evangelism." We have a message. That's our main concern. Nevertheless, there is a sense in which we *are* a message. John wrote of Jesus, "In the beginning was the Word, and the Word was with God, and the Word was God" (John 1:1). It is interesting to notice in this rather philosophical statement that Jesus is called the Word, the *logos*. John was dealing here with the challenge of communicating the gospel to both the Jews and the Greeks of his day. Nevertheless, the term *logos* does mean word. It means a verbal communication, a thought communicated in language. There is a sense in which we are that same kind of thing in the world. The fact that we are in the world is a fact that, even though no word is spoken, speaks profoundly of the truth of the gospel. If we are light, then we must shine in the world.

Jesus did not say, "You give light." Jesus rather said, "You are the light of the world" (Matt. 5:14). So we give light because we are light. Our very presence is light. Jesus also said, "You are the salt in the earth" (Matt. 5:13). This means that we are salt, that we are that which brings the quality of preserving, pungency, and flavor to a rotting, tasteless world. We must recognize that this is a unique role for the Christian in the world. He is to be somebody in the midst of a tangled world who knows the meaning of life and the answer to acceptability with God. The very fact that we are this kind of people will speak volumes even before we say a word.

Incarnational evangelism involves being somebody who is human. There is nothing wrong with being human. We must recognize that. God created human beings in the first place because he thought making man was a good idea. Since God said that man was good, we ought not to apologize for our humanness. One of the greatest blessings for Christians is to learn to be human. We must learn to share something of our humanity in order that people can see what God has done in our lives. How can anyone know what God can do through Christ to change a life unless he hears and knows something of what a changed life looks like? He needs also to know something of why a change was necessary in the first place. In other words, we need to be real. We need to be real enough to admit our mistakes and our failures, real enough to make our own human frailty a matter of testimony to God's grace and power rather than something to hide.

Incarnational evangelism has to do with that which is divine being present in the midst of that which is of the world. From a Nazi prison camp during World War II Dietrich Bonhoeffer wrote, "Just as in Christ the reality of God entered into the reality of the world, so, too, is that which is Christian to be found only in that which is of the world, the 'supernatural' only in the natural, the holy thing only in the profane, and the revelational only in the rational . . . . And yet what is Christian is not identical with what is of the world. And natural is not identical with the supernatural or the revelational and the rational. But between the two there is in each case a unity which derives solely from the reality of Christ, that is to say solely from faith in this ultimate reality" (1).

In these words Bonhoeffer has clarified for us the concept of incarnational evangelism, even though he spoke of ethics. The New Testament concept of incarnation involves the divine in the midst of the unholy and worldly. Even so, the world is not all worldly in the sense of 1 John 2 as that which the Christian is not to love. We must get hold of a new understanding of what the Bible means by *worldly* and what the meaning of a new secular society has for Christian evangelism. Perhaps we have been guilty, as Bonhoeffer suggested, of making religion a prior condition for one's coming to faith in Christ. Do we need to get a new understanding of religionless Christianity when religion is defined in terms of what a man can do through his own efforts to make himself acceptable to God?

Jesus said, "The kingdom of God is within you" (Luke 17:21). He meant that the kingdom of God was a question of submission to the will of God. Therefore, the kingdom of God, the sacred, the holy, was standing in the midst of the profane, the worldly, and the secular. The Christian shouldn't be nearly as concerned about staying out of the world as he should be about keeping the world out of him. He is to penetrate the word as salt penetrates and as light penetrates to bring the good news of Christ to that world. He is to bring that good news to a new quality of life to the life bounded by the world—a life that touches the beyond, but a life without the necessity of religion, a life which in fact negates and cancels the need for religion.

Incarnational evangelism means that Christ is not to be found only within the walls of a building where Christians worship. If that were the case, he would not be found by many. Jesus Christ must be in the shops, in the factories, in the offices, in the schools, in the stores, in the oil fields, on the streets, in the prisons, in the hospitals. He must be found wherever are found disciples of his who are light in the world, who bring a ray of hope in the midst of dark despair. Modern secular society may finally set the world free from religion in order for it to find Christ. We have defined religion as man's program of intellectual, legal, and experiential activity designed to bring himself into a position of acceptability with God. That definition of religion gives us a picture of what has been made unnecessary by the coming of Jesus Christ into the world.

A Light in the Darkness

Must man even ask the religious question? In the midst of all his felt needs he is probably not even aware of the need to be reconciled to God. One who has known nothing but darkness probably wants only to learn to cope with the darkness. It may never occur to him to cry out for the light. It may be that one of the greatest temptations for the church today is to help a person become more comfortable in the darkness rather than to bring him the light. Incarnational evangelism sees the believers walking into the presence of that darkness as the light. It is not only that we come with the word that is light in the darkness, but we come knowing that our presence as believers, members of the body of Christ, brings light into that darkness.

The only time a person in the darkness may ever think to call out for the light is when he becomes aware, through the life of some Christian around him, that there is a light. This incarnational evangelism means that believers are light wherever they are, whatever the degree of the darkness. They are the salt wherever they are, whatever the degree of rottenness and deterioration. It means that we fan out into the world as those who by our very presence bring a new quality and a new dimension and shed new light on the meaning of life.

We must recognize, though, that no one person's life can communicate the whole of the gospel. We can bring light into the darkness by our presence, but we cannot communicate the gospel of Christ by just standing there. No one's life is adequate to speak of the atoning work of Christ. It may be that through the lives we live in the midst of the darkness, a person will become aware of the fact that there is light and will cry out for it. It is at that point that we have earned the right to speak a word concerning the source of that light. But we must understand that no amount of good living or good example that we might give in the world will communicate a saving knowledge of Jesus Christ.

Jesus did not just come to be an example for us in order that we might come to God by following his example. Neither do we penetrate the world to be an example to the world so that they might come to Christ by following our example. Jesus came to communicate as the highest revelation of God and at the same time to lay down his life as atonement for our sins. We must go into the world in the same way. We must communicate the highest revelation of God. At the same time, we are willing to lay down our lives in

Christian servanthood and so to indicate that a new spirit is in the world, a new understanding of life, a new atmosphere. This is incarnational evangelism.

We may continue our analogy of light in the darkness by pointing out that there are two kinds of light—one a light that repels because of its harshness, and another that draws us to itself. I can remember that as a boy I was awakened every morning before dawn to get up for chores and dressing before the school bus arrived. This awakening came the same way every morning. The light (it seemed like a 1,000-watt bulb) on the ceiling in our room was turned on with a great flourish as my cheery mother said, "Time to get up, boys!" My brother and I would groan and turn over with our faces to the wall, pulling the cover over our heads. That kind of light, though brilliant and necessary, caused us to turn away. It hurt our eyes; it broke our peaceful sleep; it called for responsibility; it caused us to respond negatively.

We can see this negative response in John's statement that men love darkness rather than light because their deeds are evil. As we bring the light to people in the world we must not be surprised that it causes, at times, a negative response. It disturbs their peace; it unsettles their sleep. The truth of God definitely comforts the aflicted but at the same time afflicts the comfortable. In communicating the gospel we may at times have communicated very well; yet we receive a negative response. Everyone is not going to embrace the fact of his lostness and his need for coming to Christ. Nevertheless, we must learn to communicate the law and the gospel so that the light, as bright as it is, can be understood clearly.

We can give that light a warmth and a compelling attractiveness about it as we represent its warmth ourselves. Jesus has promised that he, in being lifted up as a symbol of God's love in his atoning work on the cross, will draw all men unto himself. As we preach not only the law but also the gospel and proclaim Christ lifted up before men, we will find them drawn to him by the Spirit of God through the word of the gospel. The light of truth concerning the atonement of Christ is the kind of light that warms and encourages. It melts the hardness of men. All may not be warmed and turn to him. We know that wax melts by heat, while clay hardens. That which is set in the direction of a hardening will become harder through the heat and light, while that which is melting or softening will become softer, more pliable. Only as we, as light, let our light shine, not only in life but in witness to Christ, will we discover who is open to believe and who is not.

In communicating the gospel of Christ in a tangled world, we must recognize that who we are says much to interpret what we say. Christians are distinctive in the world—light in the darkness, the salt of the earth. Our very presence is a source of light, but we are commanded as well to let our light shine to the praise of the Father (Matt. 5:16). We are witnesses of Christ and can count on the work of the Holy Spirit to give our message the wings of conviction to the heart of the hearer. Though the gospel's effectiveness is not dependent upon our excellence of presentation, it deserves the best treatment we can possibly give it. Ours is a unique task no one else will take up. But how this tangled world needs our message! "As it is written, 'How beautiful are the feet of those who bring good news!' " (Rom. 10:15).

Note

1. Dietrich Bonhoeffer, *Ethics* (New York: The Macmillan Co., 1955), pp. 198-199.

8
Applying the Great Commission

In an interview just before the National Football Conference championship, one of the quarterbacks was being questioned about the upcoming game. Most of his comments concerned the usual things you would expect to hear—strengths and weaknesses of key players, whether high or low scoring was expected, the basic styles of each team. Then he made a statement that rang with an unusual sense of confidence. "I really believe we're ready for them," he said. "We have a good game plan. The coaching staff has put together a very good game plan." That comment seemed to stand out in the interview. A good game plan—I wondered what was involved in this secret strategy for victory.

I began to imagine what might go into such a game plan. I suspect it took into consideration all the coaching staff knew about the other team—weak positions, strong ones, depth. All their defensive statistics were surely weighed. How well did they do against a passing game, a running game, different formations, different kinds of plays? What was their offensive attack? Where would they likely concentrate? Then I imagined that all football wisdom of the coaching staff would be applied to the interpretation of these factors and development of the game plan. They would know that certain principles could be trusted to hold true. Certain strategies used under certain conditions could be expected to give certain results.

What is our game plan for evangelism? Do we take a serious look at the opposition we face? Are we carefully planning a strategy that promises to be successful? What are the principles we should apply to test the wisdom of our game plan? Questions like these might be more at home with football than with evangelism. But they are nonetheless relevant to our concern for a biblical approach to bringing the good news to Christ in a tangled world. We have looked at our world. We have examined modern man—inside and out. We have analyzed and, hopefully, clarified our message. We have considered some thoughts on the effective communication of that message. Now we will take a look at some biblical principles for evaluating the wisdom of our present strategies and projecting some new ones.

A close examination of the Great Commission raises serious questions in evaluating basic strategies for evangelism. An analysis of the traditional approaches to evangelism leaves me with the gnawing suspicion that more might have been done to better respond to the original intention of the Great Commission. Are we really doing the right things? Are we enlisting and instructing our people to put their energies into the best possible use? Is our whole approach in evangelism the best that might be taken? Are we challenging our dedicated laymen sufficiently so as to stimulate a vision of what God intends to do? Most basic of all, are our approaches to evangelism actually true to the biblical principles involved in the Great Commission? Let's raise some serious questions and try to find some answers.

Aim: Conversion or Discipleship?

The first Great Commission question we want to raise concerns the primary aim of evangelism. Is evangelism basically aimed at conversion or at discipleship? If the conversion of a sinner to Christianity is itself the goal toward which evangelism presses, then that conversion will satisfy those who are seeking to evangelize. Having professed Christ as Savior, the new convert is therefore considered reached with the gospel; and the responsibility of the evangelist is thus ended. If, on the other hand, the goal and thrust of evangelism is to "make disciples" (Matt. 28:19), then the responsibility and obligation of those who would evangelize has not ended at conversion.

The primary aim of evangelism as seen in the Great Commission in Matthew 28:19-20 is discipleship rather than conversion. Four verbs are present in this passage. Three of these are participles, while only one is a command. That command is "make disciples" *(matheteusate)*. The three participles are "going" *(poreuthentes)*, "baptizing" *(baptizontes)*, and "teaching" *(dadaskontes)*. A more literal interpretation of the passage might be "Going therefore, disciple all the nations, baptizing them into the name of the Father and of the Son and of the Holy Spirit, teaching them to observe all which I commanded you." The use of these particular verb forms gives the emphasis for action to the command "Make disciples." The other verbs are supportive of this priority activity.

The three participles in this statement of the Great Commission—going, baptizing, and teaching—all represent the continuing activity of the church toward the primary aim of making disciples. The first participle, going, emphasizes the scattered church in its penetration of the community, even the entire world, with the gospel of Christ. The second participle, baptizing, emphasizes the conversion of sinners to Christ. The third participle, teaching, emphasizes the continuing responsibility of the church to teach and encourage the obedience of every Christian to the commands of Christ.

The Great Commission, therefore, involves the full cycle of seeking a lost sinner, bringing him to a saving knowledge of Christ, and teaching him the biblical way of life in order that he might join the ranks of those who seek to reach lost sinners. The following diagram may help to clarify this picture for us. Note that the primary thrust of the commission is "Make disciples." But the continuing activity necessary to move us in that direction is going, baptizing, and teaching.

In preparation rallies for evangelistic crusades, I have often asked for a show of hands from those who were given significant personal help in the beginning stages of their Christian lives. I have asked which of them had some mature Christian come along to suggest that it would be good if they could get together for prayer, for Bible study, for going to share Christ with some friend, or for just talking about the Lord and the Christian walk. The response to this question has been very consistent. Only about two or three out of a hundred raise their hands to say that someone came along at their conversion to offer this kind of help. Most of us would have to admit that our experience has been just the opposite. After we've come to Christ, most of us have been expected to get all that we needed through the education program of the church or through our own personal study, with very little guidance as to what that study ought to include. The personal aspect of discipleship was missing. The price of time and effort was not paid.

Follow-through is a fundamental principle in athletics, whether in swinging at a baseball, hitting a golfball, or passing a football. The aim is not merely to swing *to* the ball, but to swing *through* it. The best approach is to swing through with a smooth continuing motion beyond contact with the ball. The question of aiming for converts or for disciples might be likened to the question of whether to swing at the ball in a chopping, halting fashion or with a smooth follow-through. Our task is to begin to introduce a person to Jesus Christ with a realization that once he accepts Christ as his Savior, his relationship with God has only begun. We must continue to introduce him to Jesus Christ in an ever-growing fashion. Looking at our responsibility this way, we begin to see those to whom we witness as potential disciples rather than merely potential converts.

The Curse of Conversionism

An emphasis upon conversion itself as the end purpose of evangelism contradicts biblical truth at several points. We are dealing here with one of the most serious problems we face as we evaluate our evangelism in light of Great Commission principles. We must learn to overcome the tendency to see conversion as an end in itself. I believe the problem is serious enough that we should give it special attention at this point. Let's sketch some of the fallacies of "conversionism" as opposed to the Great Commission evangelism.

First, conversionism denies the basic reality of the fallen nature of man. Conversion, as the initial act of turning to Christ, is but the beginning of the Christian life. That life will be marked by a continuous struggle between the flesh and the spirit, the old nature and the new nature, the old man and the new man, the carnal nature and the spiritual nature. An emphasis on conversion as the end of evangelism seems to imply that all God has in mind for the transformation of the believer takes place at conversion. Biblical understanding and experience as well indicate that this is not in reality the way things are.

A second criticism of conversionism is that it denies the need of a new Christian for a knowledge of the Scriptures. At conversion, the believer enters upon a life for which he is largely unprepared. Though the dynamic change that is brought about in regeneration radically reorients his entire life, he is not automatically equipped with a full understanding of the nature of the Christian life. He is ignorant of so many things about prayer, the importance of the Bible, how to share his faith, his relationship with the body of Christ, how to walk in the Spirit, the continual cleansing effectiveness of the blood of Christ, and so many other important concepts for everyday living. It is sad but probably true that the vast majority of Christians were not initially taught these very basic truths. Yet they were considered evangelized and, therefore, fully competent to enter into the daily struggle of the Christian life with some assurance of success. There is no less need today than there was in the first century for the pattern followed by the early believers. "They devoted themselves to the apostles' teaching and to the fellowship, to the breaking of bread and to prayer" (Acts 2:42).

Third, conversionism is also a denial of the purpose of God for the believer. It is the will of God that men should be converted to Christ. But that is only the beginning of what God intends. The apostle Paul wrote that "those God foreknew he also predestined to be conformed to the likeness of his Son, that he might be the firstborn among many brothers" (Rom. 8:29). It is the purpose of God that every believer is becoming like Jesus. He is to be growing in Christlikeness, in fruitfulness, in a continually greater dependence upon the grace of God. Great Commission evangelism will give the believer a good start toward this kind of growth. A reasonable period of orientation into the radical new life-style called the Christian life is necessary in order that the purpose of God be honored.

What we have been discussing might be called philosophical conversionism. This is a basic conviction that conversion is itself the end of evangelism. Those who hold this view see no responsibility at all beyond sharing a witness of Christ to people wherever they can be found. No follow-up is attempted. No effort is made to identify converts with the church. Compared with the total number of Christians trying to do the work of evangelism, those who hold this view are proportionately few.

A much more serious problem than philosophical conversionism is what we might call practical conversionism. This condition occurs when we say we believe in discipleship, yet our plans and priorities look like we do not. It is the age-old problem of believing one thing and doing something else. Our intentions may be good, but a significant majority of evangelical churches have no effective program for discipleship among new converts. Even though there may be new-member classes and deacon family care assignments within the church program, the actual practice in most cases is sadly lacking.

It may well be that practical coversionism is the number one contributor to the large proportion of inactive and uninvolved church members among evangelical groups. Southern Baptists, the largest evangelical denomination, record a total membership of 12.7 million. Of that number, we frankly admit that only 9.2 million are involved to any degree in the worship and ministry of the churches. This leaves the unhappy statistic that 3.5 million are unaccounted for.

It is conceivable that a church committed by conviction and by practice to effective discipleship among new converts would nonetheless lose some of these to a nonresident or inactive category. Nevertheless, it seems obvious that the chance for a high proportion of dropouts is much smaller when our convictions about discipleship are actually translated into consistent and effective action. It might be well if there were a box in the reporting blanks for the year's records which asks for the percentage still active of those new converts who were received during the previous year.

Another misconception that contributes to this problem is the idea that follow-up equals baptism or that baptism equals follow-up.

Either way, it comes out the same. This is the notion that the follow-up victory has been won when we get a new convert into the baptismal waters. We dust our hands with delight and rejoice that the new convert really meant business with God and is now well on his way toward a fruitful Christian life. Though baptism is a vital demonstration of one's confession of faith in Christ, it does not impart any magical staying power. The new convert is still but a babe in Christ and in serious need of the help, encouragement, and training that is a part of what we understand by discipleship.

Goals: Congregation or Harvest Fields?

A second Great Commission question concerns the goals that the church has for reaching people with the gospel of Christ. Will the goals for evangelism be based on the congregation or on the harvest fields? If the goals are based primarily on the fellowship of believers, the local congregation itself, those goals will reflect some desire to increase that congregation by bringing additional people into it. The vision of leaders who set the goals on that basis will be primarily the vision of a larger congregation. They will look at the size of the flock and wonder whether a 10 percent or 15 percent increase this year would be an acceptable evangelistic goal.

If, on the other hand, the basis for setting goals for evangelism is the harvest field, the congregation will focus its attention on the community rather than on the congregation. A church that looks to evangelism as primarily a means of insuring church growth denies the very nature of the Great Commission. Jesus made it clear in the parables of the lost sheep, the lost coin, and the lost son that it is those lost ones which are the concern of the Father's heart. We are not to ask, "How many are in the fold, and how many more would be a respectable increase?" We are rather to ask, "How many are yet outside the fold, and how shall we bring them in?" A church with a missionary heart will always find itself growing because its vision is for the fields.

Direction: Come or Go

A third Great Commission question that needs to be raised concerns the movement to bridge the gap between the insiders and the outsiders, those who know Christ and those who need to hear the message. The question may be phrased like this: Will the direction of evangelism be *come*, or will it be *go*? Come evangelism exerts its primary energies in seeking to get the outsider to come to the church, to revival services, to a crusade, to the Christians, in order that he may "come under the sound of the gospel." Go evangelism, on the other hand, seeks to send the believers to the outsider to bring the gospel to him wherever he is.

Several major issues need to be raised at this point. One concerns how much can be expected from the outsider. Is the responsibility for evangelism really to be left with an unbeliever who is called upon to come to a meeting where he can hear the gospel? If he refuses to come to such a meeting because he is spiritually insensitive, is he then to be blamed for the failure of that evangelism? Is the outsider's failure to carry his responsibility for evangelism a major problem in today's evangelistic success? Or, on the other hand, should we expect the primary responsibility to be carried by the believer? Is it his responsibility to go to the unbeliever and, therefore, bridge the gap between them? Is he the one who must establish communication so that the good news can be shared?

Which of the two, insider or outsider, are we most likely to be able to mobilize for bridging the communication gap? Which of the two do we have more influence upon? Which of the two is likely to be more motivated to move toward the other so that the message can be shared? Which of the two is commanded by the Lord himself to do the going? These basic questions concerning come or go evangelism will determine a great deal as to the strategy within the local church for reaching the community for Christ. How much does the shepherd expect of a lost sheep in the task of returning him to the fold? Does he stand out on the mountainside, and shout an invitation, "Come to the meeting; everybody else is here"? Is the lost sheep only to be rescued if he is present in the fold?

If come evangelism is the primary strategy, then the church will exert its greatest energies in seeking to persuade the people of the community to come to the church building to hear the gospel. If go evangelism is the primary strategy, then the church will assemble in its building primarily for the training and strengthening of the believing congregation. Its primary thrust for evangelism will be to send the believers out in a penetration of the entire community to

find those outsiders with whom they can share the good news of
Christ. The energies of the church will be exercised in motivating,
mobilizing, equipping, and supporting the members of the church
in their going so that the work of making disciples may be done.

Intention: Random Sampling or Systematic Penetration?

A fourth Great Commission question concerns the intention of
the church in reference to evangelism. Is the intention of the church
to take a random sampling of the harvest or to do a thorough and
systematic penetration of the harvest field? We usually describe
those outsiders we hope to reach as *prospects*. They are classified
in something of the same fashion as a salesman classifies prospects.
Some are those who are interested, the "good" prospects. Others
are just "fair" prospects because they have little interest in the
gospel. Then there are the "poor" prospects who are especially
worldly or may be hostile to our group. In any given community,
then, the list of "good" prospects may be fairly limited. So we
must ask whether the church intends to go into all the world or
whether it intends to sample the harvest field here and there to find
those prospects who can best benefit the ongoing life of the congregation.

I have been impressed with the fact that the mission of the church
in the world is somewhat similar to guerrilla warfare. The different
strategies that have emerged in this era of revolution and counter-revolution
may serve as a descriptive analogy for some of the strategies
for evangelism that we as churches have adopted.

The *enclave strategy* was especially prominent at one point in
Vietnam. This approach is to fortify a village in the midst of hostile
territory and hold it against the enemy. This strategy requires
the enemy combatants to surrender and be received into the secured
village in order to become a part of "our side." We may from time
to time see the enclave strategy in evangelism. In this approach, the
believers huddle together in the midst of hostile territory and occasionally
send out small bands to scout the immediate area for signs
of the enemy. This is the *withdrawal* approach, which has been
advocated from time to time since the second century. Sometimes
this approach is manifested in a "they-know-where-the-church-is"
attitude about winning the lost. Other times it is seen in a subtle,

unspoken attitude of satisfaction with the size and makeup of the congregation as it is, without any newcomers.

The enclave strategy keeps the activity within the safe perimeters of the church facilities. If any evangelism is to be done, it must be done within the secured zone. We are familiar with this approach in the use of such statements as "bringing the lost under the sound of the gospel." We may also see this in the sense of inadequacy felt by many laymen who feel it necessary to bring any friends they want to influence for Christ to the pastor of the church so that he may win them to salvation. The enclave approach considers conversion as something that, except in rare cases such as the deathbed situation, must take place "down the aisle" to the prayer altar at the front of the auditorium.

A strategy at the other extreme is the *pacification* approach. In military terms this approach seeks to use civilian personnel to teach, assist, and propagandize the local villagers and farmers in order to win them over to support for "our side." The pacification strategy in evangelism is aimed at having a major influence on the entire community in every fashion possible. This is the approach which seeks to make the community a better place to live, perhaps without really dealing with the basic issue of reconciliation with God. *Evangelism* becomes a broad term used to describe almost anything the church sets out to do. *The gospel* becomes a broad term for anything that is not contradictory to basic biblical truth.

Another approach in countering guerrilla warfare is called the *search and destroy* strategy. This approach involved sending out patrols of men for the sole purpose of finding enemy combatants to destroy. The important thing in this approach was the body count, the number of the enemy which had been killed. The search and destroy method in evangelism is that which sends out Christians to win souls, only to leave them in the field and return to give a body count. This approach may involve well-trained workers and a highly motivated strike force. Its primary emphasis is upon the number of individuals who can be chalked up as converts, whether they are ever significantly involved in the church or personal discipleship at all.

Another military strategy is the *clear and hold* approach. In this approach, a particular area would be cleared of enemy activity and held secure by strong and vigilant watchfulness. Boundary lines would be identified, established, and maintained with constant vigilance. The goal is to continually clear and hold further territory until the enemy is pushed farther and farther back and thereby overcome.

In the clear and hold strategy for evangelism, the church will identify a specific section of the community which will be saturated with a witness for Christ. Records will be kept on those who live in that section until each home is clearly identified as to the relationship to Christ of those within it. Goals may be set concerning the specific number of blocks that will be reached during a given year.

The church will continue to expand the territory while maintaining a knowledge of any changes within that area. Over a period of several years this section-by-section advance may lead to a saturation of the gospel in the entire community. As each section is secured, block captains will be assigned to maintain a constant awareness of new people who move in and any changes in the situation in homes of already-established families.

In Acts 1:8 Jesus' commission is framed in terms of the systematic penetration of an ever-enlarging area. He begins by saying that the believers would be witnesses of his in the local community, Jerusalem. From there he moves to the larger geographical unit surrounding the community, the region of Judea. The ever-enlarging scope of the witness penetration then moves to the adjacent region, Samaria. Having established the pattern of a systematic and progressive enlargement of the area of evangelistic concern, Jesus gives the ultimate aim of his commission—"unto the remotest corner of the earth."

If the church intends to do a systematic saturation of the entire community, then the goals it sets will not be in terms of the congregation. If goals are set in terms of the harvest field, those goals will probably begin with how many workers must be trained in order to saturate the entire community. The goals may be in terms of how many houses will be reached within a certain period of time rather than how many attractive visitors will be enlisted for the church meetings. When a church fully expects to do a saturation outreach in the entire community, plans will need to be made for reaching every home in the community, a section at a time.

The basic strategy of the church for evangelism will not only shape the character of the congregation but determine priorities for every phase of its ministry. On the one hand is the church which hopes year after year to reach a number based on an increase in the present size of the congregation. Its vision for evangelism will be determined by the strength and resources of the church. On the other hand is the church that develops a plan for evangelism based on a systematic penetration of the entire community. Its vision for evangelism will be based on the expectation of presenting the gospel to every person in its designated territory.

The Christian: Salesman or Witness?

Another Great Commission question which needs to be raised concerns the character of the believer's task. Is the Christian who would do the work of evangelism to be characterized as a witness or as a salesman? A witness is one who shares what he has seen or heard and knows from firsthand knowledge to be true. A salesman would, or course, be one who is out to make a sale, to convince someone to purchase his product. At the point of the actual sharing of the message, the Great Commission emphasis is upon being witnesses. The thrust of the Great Commission in Matthew 28:19-20 is to make disciples. A disciple is a learner or pupil who receives the teachings and instructions of his master. It is in the very nature of discipleship to call for the willingness and receptive spirit of the hearer.

Jesus said, "You will be my witnesses" (Acts 1:8). A witness is one who shares information he knows personally to be true. He is not obligated to prove that information true to the satisfaction of the hearer. Jesus' parable of the sower and the seed indicates that the word of God may be sown on all kinds of ground. But the character of the type of ground will determine the fruitfulness of the seed. The sower cannot force a positive response where the soil is not receptive. It is the word of God that is the living and powerful discerner of the thoughts and plans of a man's heart (Heb. 4:12). It is the Spirit who convinces the unbeliever of sin, righteousness, and judgment (John 15:8), and exalts Christ (John 15:26).

In some quarters there has for years been the "super soul saver" motif, which pictures the soul-winner as a clever and persuasive salesman. He knows all the objections and has a ready answer for each one. He knows tricky ways to get into a man's house, turn off his television set, control the conversation, and get him to make some kind of response, if only reaching out to take his hand. We have already noted in our discussion of faith that being converted is not something one decides to do out of merely rational and volitional processes. Coming to Christ is a spiritual transaction which awaits a divine call and spiritual enabling.

A person may well come to Christ in the context of a pressure sales pitch. But the emphasis of Great Commission evangelism is upon the Spirit-empowered sharing of the gospel message. The faithfulness of a witness is not measured by the response of the hearer but by the truth of the message and the honesty of the report. God reserves to himself the right to call whom he will and leaves the hearer the right to embrace or refuse his call.

It is evident from the terms in Acts describing the evangelistic ministry of Paul that the apostle was a forceful and persuasive preacher (Acts 9:29; 17:2; 18:4; 19:8,26,28). The Christian must seek to bear the message in the most skillful and persuasive manner possible. Nevertheless, the burden of making a sale is not his. He will hope to see a person respond in a faith commitment to Christ. He knows, though, that no amount of reasoning, persuading, arguing, or cajoling will of itself bring a response of conviction, repentance, and faith. That response comes only as the Spirit of God works through the word of God to do the work of a divine Salesman.

Message: the Church or Jesus?

A sixth Great Commission question concerns the basic evangelistic message of the church. Is the message one concerning the church, its ministry, its services, and its benefits, or does the evangelistic message concern Jesus Christ himself and the hearer's relationship to him? The church's construction of its message reveals much about its beliefs: What is man's basic need? What is the best contribution the church can make toward the meeting of that need? What unique role among other institutions is the church to play in the community? What kind of response must come from the people in the community for the church to consider its message received?

The message a church is declaring can be observed in its visitation outreach and in any advertising the church may do. What do the church visitors talk about when they call on homes of unbelievers in the community? Do they share the benefits of the church? Do they tell about the pastor, the Sunday School, the church program? If the content of a visitor's conversation never touches on the gospel of Christ, can we conclude that he sees the Christian message in other terms? If the church advertises in newspapers, on radio, or with posters in the community, what is the message it presents? Does that reflect the basic message of the church?

We have already discussed the nature and content of the gospel of Christ. We have sketched the relationship between testimony and gospel. We have also dealt with the challenge of communicating that gospel. To be most effective in our communication we must catch man's attention at a point where he senses a need. It may well be that the church in its institutional ministry has a story of real interest to the community. But that story must not be substituted for the gospel of Christ, which is the power of God unto salvation.

Worship: For unbelievers or Christians?

A seventh Great Commission question concerns the purpose of the worship meetings of the church. Are the worship services primarily designed to present an opportunity for those present to receive Christ—that is, evangelism? On the other hand, are the worship sessions designed to help strengthen, edify, and teach those present for the living of the Christian life? The concept the church leadership has of evangelism will be reflected in this aim for the worship services. What is the primary aim of the pastor's sermons? What criteria do we use to judge whether we had a good service? Is our evangelism going to take place primarily inside the building?

Many a service is begun with a prayer that should there be those present who need to receive Christ, they will come to him that day. This is a worthy concern. Our prayer should always be that any seekers present may come to Christ. But there seems to be a weak understanding of evangelism reflected in a prayer based on *if* there happen to be any unsaved present. Many of our laymen have been taught to see evangelism as that which takes place in the regular worship or revival services of the church. They have understood that it is here that the lost must come under the sound of the gospel.

It is a sad situation when a pastor stands week after week to preach a sermon designed for the lost multitudes who are not present. The value of the gospel message seems cheapened when an evangelistic invitation is pressed to a congregation of regular church members. This situation very often leaves the congregation with a sense of frustration and embarrassment. No one was there to receive Christ, and those who did hear the message had no particular benefit from it. In this kind of situation the matchless gospel of Christ is in danger of becoming common, dull, and irrelevant to the congregation. Hearing it so often with little apparent effect does not encourage enthusiasm for the message of salvation.

Would it not be ridiculous for the commanding officer of a group of army recruiters to urge them with impassioned tones to join the army? Would it not be ridiculous for a sales manager to plead with his salesmen to buy the product they are seeking to sell? Is it not just about as ridiculous for a pastor to plead week after week for someone to come to Christ out of the midst of a congregation of believers who have already made that basic commitment? They need now to hear the nourishing message of the Word, which will equip and edify them for taking that message into the community at large. Shouldn't we do our fishing out on the lake where the fish are, rather than trying to get those in the bucket to take the hook again?

Should not the basic thrust of the worship be for the Christian? Can a worship service be for anyone but believers who alone can truly worship? Will the unbelievers who are present not understand something of the Christian life and the gospel by hearing a biblical message designed to strengthen believers? Cannot such a message be easily turned to an evangelistic invitation and thus meet the needs of both groups? It is often the churches where preaching is designed to "feed the sheep" that have the greatest number of lost persons in the services. The church where Christians are really growing becomes warm and enthusiastic. It is this kind of church that attracts the interest of Christians and seekers alike.

But let's not equate this kind of preaching ministry with the dull, academic approach some have taken. It is not necessary for a church to encourage either Christian growth or evangelism. An emphasis upon either need should never be an excuse for neglecting the other. A New Testament church will be doing both. The preaching ministry of the pastor will do much to set the tone of the congregation's outlook and shape the evangelistic character of the church.

These Great Commission questions, as difficult to answer as they are, are not raised to suggest that we scrap traditional approaches to evangelism. They are raised to stimulate a practical search for the best and most biblically valid strategies for reaching an entire community with the gospel. Christians who are serious about the Great Commission will not be afraid to ask difficult questions. Neither will they be afraid to search anew for biblical insights for evangelism. In fact, Christian leaders must, as they face the challenge of a tangled world, return to the most basic of questions for planning strategies for evangelism.

The Great Commission questions we have raised do not lead us to all the answers for getting the good news to a tangled world. We have, though, identified some choices for the church in formulating its strategies for evangelism. Let's review them:

1. Will the end of evangelism be seen as conversion or discipleship?

2. Will evangelistic goals be based on the size of the congregation or on the needs of the harvest field?

3. Will the movement to reach the lost be conceived in terms of *come* evangelism or *go* evangelism?

4. Will the intention of the church be to take a random sampling of the harvest or to do a systematic penetration of the entire community with the gospel?

5. Will the believer be characterized in the mind of the church as a salesman or as a witness for Christ?

6. Will the outreach message concern the church and its ministry or Christ and his work of salvation?

7. Will the meetings of the church be designed primarily for equipping the believers or evangelizing the unbelievers who may be there?

Planning for Evangelism

How, then, will a church plan for effective evangelism? We have examined some principles that will guide our thinking. Now let's apply them in a consideration of steps for the planning of an overall strategy for bringing good news to a tangled world. These steps will include: (1) setting measurable goals, (2) developing a plan for attaining the goals, (3) formulating work assignments for implementing the plan, (4) selecting and preparing workers to accept the assignments,

(5) determining procedures for a periodic review of progress.

First, careful study and thought must be given to the setting of measurable goals, the absence of which leads to a lack of direction and progress in evangelism. These goals should be measurable in terms of time. Long-range goals should be projected. Then these goals must be broken down into intermediate and short-range goals. Goals should also be measurable in terms of quantity. They should be phrased in terms of precise and concrete figures. Goals should also be measurable in terms of quality. Mimimum acceptable standards of quality should be applied before a goal is considered reached.

The goals must be true to the most fundamental principles of biblical evangelism. If we set a goal for so many baptisms, what does this say about the priority of discipleship? If we set a goal based on a percentage increase of the congregation, what does this say about the focus of biblical evangelism on the field? If our goals are based on the number of people we can gather in an evangelistic meeting, what does this say about the "going" thrust of the Great Commission? If our goals are based on reaching so many prospects, what does this say about the biblical mandate for a systematic penetration of the world with the gospel? Goals should reflect the commitment of the church to the fulfillment of the Great Commission.

A church may want to set goals for the area of the community it expects to reach within five years. Then graduated goals for each year will be derived from that long-range goal. From the yearly goals, monthly and weekly goals can be set. If the aim is communitywide saturation with the gospel, goals will be needed for an increasing number of trained, witnessing disciples for that work. Goals will be needed for upgrading and enlarging the Bible-teaching ministry of the church in order to properly minister to the new believers. Goals may also be projected for the personal growth of the congregation in the kinds of strengths that characterize a warm, vibrant fellowship. Goals will also be set for measuring the effectiveness of various programs which make up the overall plan.

The second step of planning is the development of a plan for attaining evangelistic goals. Setting goals without making definite plans for reaching them is like daydreaming—it has little to do with reality. We must always ask upon the setting of any goal, "Upon what basis can we hope to reach this goal?" Plans that are precisely designed to reach our goals must be developed. An overall "game plan" for evangelism may include several programs. We may plan for witness training, renewal emphases, discipleship classes, saturation canvassing, prospect visitation, revival meetings, media evangelism, target group evangelism, neighborhood block plans, child evangelism projects, and so forth. But we must carefully evaluate the strengths, weaknesses, and compatibility of these programs.

In developing a comprehensive game plan, we must always keep our goals in mind. In our enthusiasm, it is easy to "ride off in all directions." We must honestly evaluate the potential of each program for contributing to our goals. We must weigh it by the measure of biblical principles. We must determine the resources and personnel available for any given program. We must establish priorities and begin with those programs which deserve the highest priority. We must avoid the clutter of too many concurrent programs. It is better to do a few things well than many things poorly. We must take into careful consideration the nature of the particular community. All in all, our purpose is to develop a workable plan by which we can fully expect to reach our goals.

A third step in planning involves translating into work assignments the various programs that make up our game plan. We must determine what work needs to be done to implement each program. We must divide that into assignments made up of particular tasks and responsibilities. Churches have often made positions of honor out of church leadership responsibilities. They have been responsibilities in name only. All too often no job description is provided. No specific tasks are spelled out. The person accepting the position is never quite sure how well he's doing because he doesn't know what he's agreed to do. We must avoid this kind of vagueness. Responsibilities and tasks should be spelled out specifically in a form that leaves no uncertainty as to the assignment.

A fourth step in planning involves the selection and preparation of workers for each responsibility. As these are enlisted each one should clearly understand the overall goals, the plan for reaching them, the various programs which make up that plan, and his particular part in the whole picture. If a person is unable to agree to the tasks as they are outlined, he should not be asked to take the assignment. If the job description can be altered without compromising its purpose, this may be done. Otherwise, a different person must be found for the job. The worker should understand who will be in his project group, those for whose work he is responsible, and the one to whom he is to look for leadership.

A fifth step in planning for evangelism is the determining of procedures for a periodic review of progress. Unless we check regularly whether we are moving toward our goals, there is little use setting goals. It is characteristic of man to "go astray, turning every one to his own way" (Isa. 53:6). Unless the lines of communication are kept open and frequently used, a worker may lose sight of the goal and stray off the path of his assignment. It is vital that someone be assigned to assist that worker in whatever ways are necessary so that he may do well the job he has agreed to do. He will need guidance, encouragement, resources, understanding, support, and the awareness that someone is expecting him to report on his progress. This review of the progress of each worker, each project, and each program will provide a means of knowing at any time whether we are on target and on schedule. We cannot correct our courses when revision is needed unless we are aware of getting off course.

We have examined the Great Commission to learn principles for effective evangelism. We have looked at our own approaches to evangelism in light of these principles. We have proposed steps for planning and implementing a game plan for bringing the good news to a tangled world. Many questions remain. Most of these will be answered in the laboratory of prayerful, earnest involvement in the fulfillment of the Great Commission. Let us be going, baptizing, and teaching that we may make disciples, even to the farthest corner of the earth.

9
Keys to Motivation

Some of the funniest old movie sketches I've ever seen had their setting at a dude ranch. The situation is full of possibilities for hilarious comedy. There are the "city slickers" and other nonranch types dressed up in exaggerated cowboy garb—stumblesome boots, oversized western hats, decorated chaps, vests, and bandanas. They are all assembled at the dude ranch for a time of make-believe cowboy life. There's always the hilarious scene with the dressed up "dude" trying to mount a horse for the first time. He goes all the way over the saddle a couple of times and finally winds up mounted facing backward. It's all for fun for a make-believe weekend in the old west.

I recently was struck with the thought that there may be an analogy between the dude ranch and some expressions of the church today. But that is not very funny. Is the church a dude ranch where weekend cowboys come to hang around the bunkhouse? Or is it a real working farm where the hands come by for instructions and tools but know that their real job is in the fields? This is one of the biggest challenges for evangelism today—getting out of the bunkhouse. It seems that for many (or most) of our most committed believers the Sunday experience inside the church building is about the extent of their Christian service.

What is closest to the heart of God in the work of the church? What is closest to the mission of Christ? Is it not the point of contact for God's redemptive work today? Is it not that point where the salvation grace of God meets the needs of lost humanity? Isn't that thing closest to the heart of God the conversion of a sinner to

Christ? What else is the church doing that evokes the rejoicing of the angels in heaven? Jesus' parables of the lost sheep, the lost coin, and the lost son make clear the priority for evangelism (Luke 15).

Christians today have learned to substitute "church work" for the work of the church. Christian maturity is measured more in terms of tenure than spiritual growth. The really mature church members are the ones most familiar with the inhouse routine, the ones who know where all the light switches are. There are multitudes of deacons, Bible teachers, and other church officers held in high esteem by the congregation who have never once been personally involved in evangelism. Their participation in the redemptive mission of the church is like that of the spectators in the stands of a football game. They watch every play, cheer the successes, and bemoan the losses, but are never actually a part of the game. They are part of the going without getting out, part of the witnessing without saying a word, part of the victory without entering the real battle.

What is the reason for this prevailing view of evangelism as a "spectator sport"? Could it be the idea that the pastor and staff are to do the soul-winning? Could it be that few have ever really pressed the issue? Could it be, as one layman said, that the pastor continually urges them to be witnesses but seldom actually shows them how? Could it be that the priorities of the church do not place evangelism in a primary position, that the church is more concerned with such things as its buildings, facilities, and financial obligations? Could it be that most of our evangelism is institutional rather than individual? Could it be that witnessing has not been pictured as normal to the Christian life but supernormal and extraordinary—reserved for dynamic disciples a cut above the regular troops?

Maybe all these factors have entered in to maintain the condition whereby the church can seem to get along quite well without significant outreach. An evangelical church may actually be more embarrassed at a failure to meet its budget requirements than at a failure to see men won to Christ. There is the temptation to maintain a "business as usual" stance for the sake of respectability. No reason to panic. No cries of alarm. Except for a bit of dust in the baptistry, the church is doing quite well. So our problem remains how to motivate and mobilize the believers for the work of penetrating the entire community with the gospel of Christ.

The Basic Elements of Evangelism

Writers in recent years have called our attention to the concept of the *gathered church* and the *scattered church*. The gathered church is the body of Christ come together for worship, inspiration, encouragement, mutual support, prayer, instruction, and equipment for the work of the ministry. The scattered church is the body at large in the community, ministering, witnessing, caring, functioning as the salt of the earth and the light of the world. But the fact remains that whether gathered or scattered, much of the church is not at all significantly involved in the real task of bringing the gospel to a needy world.

There are three basic elements involved in evangelism: the message, the multitudes, and the messenger. In each of these elements God works to provide needed spiritual dynamic. We have already discussed the message, the gospel of Christ, in previous chapters. If that message is still relevant to the needs of modern man, then it must be proclaimed. If that message is still "the power of God unto salvation to every one who believes," then it must be proclaimed. If that message is the truth that casts a shadow of error over every competing answer, then it must be proclaimed. If that message is still the only finally effective answer to man's estrangement from God, then it must be proclaimed.

The second basic element in evangelism is the multitudes for whom the message is prepared. They are the objects of concern in bringing the gospel of Christ to the world. It was those whom Jesus came to seek and to save and for whom he gave his life as a ransom. I have heard it said that you can't win people to Jesus because they're not interested these days. They're hard, sophisticated, self-sufficient, and cold. They won't respond as they did in other generations. They won't come to church or revival meetings. They won't listen to our sermons. But what can we expect of the multitudes? Concerning the metaphor of Jesus' last parable of the lost sheep we might ask, what can the shepherd expect of a lost sheep? The multitudes are not expected to do anything to contribute to the evangelistic enterprise. The very fact that they are there is their part in the drama of redemption.

It is easy to miss seeing the need. Yet the multitudes are there with all their multiplicity of needs, their hungers, their yearnings, their desires. They are there with their own ideas as to what the answer may be. They are there in their brief happinesses, their tragic sorrows, in their successes, in their failures. They are there to enjoy the tenderness and love that is a part of human life, even in its fallen state. They are there with an emptiness that can be filled in no way except through the salvation that is in Christ. It is that very emptiness and need which is the contribution made by the multitudes to complete the picture of evangelism. Whether as religious man, secular man, or some other type, it is the lost multitudes who made redemption a necessary act of God's love.

The third basic element in evangelism is the messenger. The messenger brings the life-giving gospel to the lost multitudes. He is the "evangel," the bearer of the good news. We have noted that there is nothing wrong with the gospel and that nothing is expected of the multitude. So the point of our particular concern is the messenger. It is here that we face our most serious challenge. The millions of serious lay believers form a vast army of witnesses who have only been marginally involved in the task of evangelism. How we can motivate, equip, and mobilize them for the work is the subject of this chapter.

Understanding Motivation

One of the most important functions of leadership is the task of motivation. There is a direct relationship between our performance and our inspiration or enthusiasm for the work. So few of us are self-starters who need no incentive or encouragement. To the contrary, most of us are plagued with apathy and indifference. Unless a task has directly to do with our personal survival, we are likely to approach it in an offhanded, disinterested manner. Unfortunately, the task of evangelism faces these same problems. There is a constant need to keep the inspiration up, to reinspire the saints with an impulse to bring the gospel to a needy community.

Evangelical churches have attempted an interesting variety of approaches to motivating people for evangelism. We have made them promise with soul-winning commitment cards. We have shamed them in rousing sermons. We have given them the names of unbelievers. We have scheduled evangelistic services, packed the pews, signed the bananas to be "one of the bunch," and worked to reach goals. We have scheduled soul-winning courses, formed "fishermen's clubs," taken surveys, and planned visitation nights. There is no doubt we have tried to motivate our people for evangelism.

Let's note, though, the meaning of motivation. The word *motive* comes from a Latin verb meaning to move. We are not surprised at that. But an important idea is built in to the meaning of motivation. A motive is actually something *within* the individual rather than without. It is something inside—an idea, a need, an emotion, a loyalty—that incites him to action. So a motive in the truest sense of the word cannot be extrinsic, from outside the person. It must be intrinsic, from within. Of course, motives are developed through outside influences. Otherwise leaders could never be motivators. To be a motivator, a leader provides the individual with a motive that continues to inspire from within. Our approach to motivation must not be the carrot-on-a-stick approach so much as an effort to stimulate a desire within that becomes a part of the person's concept of himself.

Our guide for understanding appropriate motivation for evangelism is the Scripture itself. We can particularly see in Jesus' ministry his ability to inspire men to unusual effort and sacrifice. In the remainder of this chapter we will examine ten insights for motivation which can be seen in the ministry of Christ. These ideas are practical and expecially relevant for the challenge of getting the good news to a tangled world.

Following the Leader

Jesus was himself a source of motivation for those who were with him. His commitment to the purpose of God inspired a similar commitment in his disciples. His priorities gave them a sense of value. As disciples they followed him through the villages and towns on his itinerary. They listened to him teach. They obeyed his instructions. They participated in his ministry. They became like him. As much as his teachings or his mighty works, they were impressed with the man himself. They ultimately reflected his character, his burden, his outlook on life.

The apostle Paul seemed at times to lose his humility in asserting the effectiveness of his own example. To the believers at Corinth he plainly declared, "Therefore I urge you to imitate me" (1 Cor. 4:16). How many of us in places of leadership would be so bold as to offer that instruction? Lest we misunderstand Paul, let's note two more statements. Paul encouraged the Philippians, "Join with others in following my example, brothers, and take note of those who live according to the pattern we gave you" (Phil. 3:17). But the most comprehensive statement of all in this vein is this exhortation: "Whatever you have learned or received or heard from me, or seen in me—put it into practice. And the God of peace will be with you" (Phil. 4:9). That is almost too much for us to absorb. Not only does he give final authority to his teachings but to his own life as a worthy example.

We must recognize in these statements of Paul an awareness of the crucial role of leadership in the church. The leaders of God's people are not only to be imaginative planners and efficient administrators but also they are to be examples worthy of emulation. My daddy used to say in jest, "Son, don't do as I do; do as I say do!" But there is no place for an inconsistency of walk and talk among God's leaders. Like it or not, the people will reflect their leaders. If a pastor's priorities are finances and buildings, the people will accept that as proper. If his heart is burdened for reaching the community for Christ, they will accept that. Whatever is reflected in his life, his words, his attitudes, his teaching will become the outlook of the church; and that overall perspective becomes itself a source of motivation.

Facing the Real Need

Another vital source of motivation is a graphic first-hand awareness of the needs of people without Christ. Matthew wrote that as Jesus went about through all the towns and villages, he saw the multitudes in their need and had compassion on them (Matt. 9:35-36). Jesus saw them as harassed and helpless, like sheep without a shepherd" (Matt. 9:36). He saw them as they were—fainting (*eskulmenoi*), vexed, and bewildered, scattered *(errimmenoi)*, cast down, and dejected. He saw their need because he was out among these multitudes. He was moved with compassion because of his shepherd's heart, because he saw the significance of their plight from God's viewpoint. Any apparent happiness, affluence, or prominence did not veil their true need.

Our difficulty today is the secular idea that men are getting along very well without God. But we must expose our people to the truth. We must lead them through the battlefields and let them see the casualties. Perhaps they need to sit through a few divorce proceedings. Perhaps they need to talk with narcotics officers. Perhaps they need to visit the mental wards. Perhaps they need a guided tour to some of the bars, X-rated movie houses, and adult bookstores. We do not have to be experts on sin to know that men need Christ. Our point is that many middle-class American Christians could well be unaware of the reality of the needs about them.

It is not until we lift up our eyes to see the fields that we cry out to the Lord of the harvest for workers. If our attention is upon the activity that takes place in the relative security of our church buildings, we may see no need for more workers. But when we see the multitudes as they really are, we realize how poorly staffed our churches are for the task of evangelism. We do not have a shortage of "good" people or worship attenders, but "the workers are few" (Matt. 9:37). In the sheltered well-being of church work, they tend to forget the real work of the church. We must awaken their awareness of reality and bring them abruptly back in contact with the way things actually are in a fallen world. Then we must interpret that reality to them in terms of the gospel.

The Joy of Knowing How

Another key motivation for evangelism is knowing how to share Christ personally. In Jesus' almost constant fellowship with his disciples, he showed them how to declare the gospel of the kingdom to the multitudes of his day. They learned the basic message, the response that was necessary, and the attitude they were to have as they ministered. Jesus gave detailed instructions to the twelve and the seventy as he sent them into the towns where he was about to go (Luke 9; 10). He told them to expect hostility, travel lightly, stick to their business, associate with supporters, accept hospitality, heal the sick, preach the kingdom of God is near, and not let the dust of unrepentant towns cling to their feet. He obviously wanted them to know well how to fulfill the task.

If our aim is to see a maximum mobilization of laymen for the task of personal witnessing, we must recognize that preaching alone is not all they need to stimulate them. We must not only press the responsibility of every believer for personal evangelism; we must also provide training in how to do it. Many a pastor has already learned that a witnessing class is not enough in itself. There must be the practical training which comes with actual experience. In a sharing meeting following a lay witness training school, several of the participants shared what I didn't expect. Their most emphatic comment concerned how good it was to know how to share Christ effectively at any time. What a joy—knowing you know how.

Getting Under the Load

Another effective motivator is a share in the responsibility for the work. So many laymen have never really felt a responsibility for the evangelistic outreach of the church. This is seen as the pastor's job. He is to carry the load of enlisting, training, motivating, and sending out the lay witnesses. What happens when a layman becomes a trained and effective witness? He probably still expects all the push, all the sense of obligation for outreach to be borne by the pastor. But when a layman is given a share of that load, he begins to see the whole enterprise in a different light.

In sending out the twelve and the seventy, Jesus demonstrated his confidence in them. He laid a heavy load of responsibility on them. This was not a matter of following him about as he taught and ministered. They were on their own. The training had been good. The instructions were clear. Now they must get under the load of this work. They now had an investment in it of time, energy, and reputation. The success or failure of the movement was largely in their hands. They were highly motivated by this assignment and returned with joy to report their success (Luke 10:7).

So it is that when a layman gets under the burden of the church's evangelistic outreach, he becomes motivated about it. He may have been chairman of ushers, served on the building committee, or made hospital calls before. But now the work of bringing men to Christ is his. He may be involved in the training of a group of others in the same way he has been trained. He may be asked to take one man and follow a prescribed program of work in discipling him. He may be asked to accept responsibility for his neighborhood in seeing that each home is reached there within a specified period of time. Whatever the responsibility, it should be clearly spelled out. The real motivation comes in knowing exactly what is expected and realizing that the success of the work is in his hands.

A Climate of Accountability

In some churches a believer can accept a position of responsibility without ever being told what he is to do or having anyone inquire as to whether he is actually doing an acceptable job. In fact, with no job description or task assignment, there can be no unacceptable job. Since there are no requirements, any effort at all will be adequate. Some committee members serve for a year while never attending a committee meeting or clearly knowing the committee's purpose. What I am saying is that many of our churches have established a climate of irresponsibility. Rarely is a volunteer worker called on to give an accounting of his work. For this reason the effectiveness of the work is dependent on the individual rather than any established standards based on overall church purposes.

I realize that a volunteer staff of workers in a church cannot be regimented like employees in business. But I do believe that there are many serious believers who would welcome a more definite approach to their work assignments. When specific job descriptions are drawn up, specific reports required, specific standards of effectiveness spelled out, and specific structures of responsibility set up, the volunteer worker gets the idea it really makes a difference whether he does his job. As this approach is taken to the evangelistic outreach of the church, a climate of responsibility and accountability is developed. People begin to be much better motivated because they know they will be asked to give an account of their work.

It is not without significance that the seventy Jesus sent out were expected to report back to him (Luke 10:17). Jesus did not assign them this project as busywork to keep them out of mischief or to help them feel important. It was an important project at this point in his ministry. There was an earnestness about all the ministry of Jesus that fostered a sense of expectancy and responsibility. The redemptive purpose of God was a deadly serious program to Jesus. In the parables of the tower builder and the king going to war (Luke 14:28-33) he made clear that his disciples were accountable for their faithfulness and sacrifice. Since our work today is in the same redemptive purpose of God, can we be less serious about faithfulness? I believe we would often be surprised at the eagerness and motivation with which many of our people would embrace a "mean business" system of accountability in our work.

Someone to Turn To

A common reason why our lay workers often lose their zeal for a project within a relatively short time is the lack of close personal help in it. We ask someone to do a job and then turn him loose. This approach may seem to honor his integrity and dedication, but it shows a poor understanding of human nature. Our tendency is, like sheep, to go astray, to turn every one to his own way (Isa. 53:6). Without close, personal supervision periodically we will allow other things to crowd in on our time and attention and will procrastinate to the point of failure. In seeking to motivate our lay workers, we must see that they get all the continuing personal encouragement, resources, and support they need to do their work.

What we are dealing with here is the need for genuinely Christian leadership at a more personal level. We must learn to provide every worker with someone to turn to, someone whose purpose is to do all he can to insure that worker's success in his task. This concept of Christian leadership is made clear in Jesus' discussion of greatness in the kingdom (Matt. 20:20-28). He says, "Whoever wants to become great among you must be your servant, and whoever wants to be first must be your slave" (Matt. 20:26-27). Leadership or greatness is determined on the basis of one's sincere service to those for whom he is responsible.

It is a great source of motivation to know that you have a leader who is committed to your success, personally informed about the details of your work, attempting to serve you by providing every counsel, encouragement, and resource you need. This is a leader who calls you from time to time to inquire about the specifics of your work and to check on what help you may need. He is not a boss but a helper. He has few enough workers in his group that he can maintain close personal contact. When structures of leadership are conceived in these terms, the lay workers in a church will be much more likely to be faithful, efficient, and highly motivated at every level of responsibility.

The Flame of Fellowship

Another source of motivation closely related to the one above is a sense of group identity and loyalty. This is a team spirit that inspires and encourages each member of the group to do his best. So often in our church efforts at evangelism we have a "y' all come" approach to enlisting workers. We make announcements from the pulpit to press everyone to be there for Tuesday night visitation. But we know that everyone is not going to be there. We are planning on a poor response. In fact, we are programmed for it. The more we make such announcements without really expecting people to respond, the more we foster disregard for our announcements.

Jesus did not enlist his trusted disciples in a mass appeal for any and all who would like to join his team. He individually selected the twelve on the basis of the keen insight he had into their own spirits. Neither did he announce monthly apostles' meetings at the feeding of the five thousand. He rather handpicked his team, trained them, and sought to mold them into a loyal and compatible group. They had a sense of group identity. They were part of an important team. They were responsible to function as a group, to be supportive of one another, and to faithfully execute any assignments given them by Jesus.

When key laymen are selected for a specific task and joined in a small group of others involved in the same work, the team spirit begins to work. As communications are kept open and direct, as group purposes are clearly defined, as special training and expertise is provided, as priority is asked for group tasks, a high degree of motivation develops. The group experiences the flame of fellowship in a worthy cause. Some churches today are learning the value of such small action groups in a task-force approach to special project evangelism. As different workers are involved in any given evangelistic strategy, they can gain valuable support in many ways from involvemen in such a close-knit select group.

Visualizing a Worker's Potential

A valuable approach to motivation involves expressing confidence in others on the basis of God's faithfulness. This means we see a fellow worker from the viewpoint of his potential. Jesus looked at a rough fisherman named Simon and saw in him by God's grace Peter the apostle (Matt. 16:17-18). Through the inspiration of the Holy Spirit the church at Antioch saw in Saul, by God's grace, the great missionary Paul. In his letters to the saints Paul expressed confidence in their faithfulness, even in the face of evidence to the contrary

(2 Cor. 1:15; 2:3; 7:16; 8:22). His confidence was based on the faithfulness of God (Gal. 5:10; 2 Thess. 3:4). God always selects men on the basis of their potential by his grace and not on the basis of their particular gifts or performance.

This same confidence in men should be expressed by church leaders. It is not that we have any confidence in the fallen nature of man. We rather know what God can do with a man. The motivation that is evoked by these sincere expressions of confidence can be explained from several angles. It may be a sort of self-fulfilling prophecy. We place an idea in a person's mind, and he makes it a constant reference point for his decisions and actions. This is something of the power of suggestion. We stimulate a person's imagination with an image of himself as faithful and effective so that he expects it of himself. But beyond these psychological effects is the fact that God honors our faith when we express confidence in a fellow believer by his grace.

Whatever the inner mechanics of this motivation, it is effective. A climate of openness, acceptance, and confidence always gets better mileage than a critical spirit. We must accept our workers as they are rather than on the basis of their performance. If their performance is unacceptable, that does not cause us to close them out in a judgmental response. We are committed to helping them succeed in the Lord's work. We must, therefore, help determine the reason for their poor work. It may be due to too little help and encouragement, a fuzzy understanding of the job, lack of close personal contact, or a matter of being ill-suited for the particular task. We can know, though, that when we visualize his potential effectiveness with a worker, he will likely be motivated to fulfill that vision.

The Divine Motivator

In personal evangelism there is a mysterious fear and reluctance that often overtakes us. We can talk easily about anything but Jesus Christ. Only with much prayer and practice do we ever overcome this dread. Even then we may suffer relapses of it. The intensely personal nature of our witness and the implication of moral indictment built into it are part of the cause for our hesitance. On the positive side, though, is the divine motivation of the Spirit of God toward faithfulness in sharing Christ. Jesus promised that with the coming of the Spirit into their lives, the believers would receive power for being witnesses of Christ (Acts 1:8). The same Spirit that drove Jesus into the wilderness after his baptism (Mark 1:12) drives us as well toward involvement in the redemptive work of God (Rom. 8:14).

As the divine motivator, the Spirit opens our understanding to the significance of the Great Commission. As no man can do, he presses it upon us as a personal calling (Acts 13:2). He convicts us of our sin and stirs our selfish hearts with compassion for the lost (Rom. 5:5). As a co-witness with us, he honors our witness by working to persuade the sinner of the truth (Acts 5:32). He gives us boldness to speak the word of God, even in the face of threat (Acts 4:31). He gives our witness power beyond the speech and wisdom of man (1 Cor. 2:4). So he moves us and then empowers our witness as a great source of motivation for evangelism.

How can we fully cooperate with this ministry of the Spirit in encouraging our people? Of course we realize that the Spirit of God is not to be manipulated. Ours is not to use him but to allow him to use us. We must expose our people often to occasions conducive to worship. Retreats, prayer meetings, and other devotional-type meetings will offer special opportunities for the Spirit to press the task of evangelism on our people. We must encourage them to meet God daily in a quiet time of worship. We must make clear the biblical truth concerning the ministry of the Spirit. As we help our people learn to walk in the Spirit, we will see them divinely motivated for that work closest to God's heart.

A Vision and a Burden

In the Lamentations, Jeremiah described the woeful state of God's people in captivity. At one point he said, "Also her prophets find no vision from the Lord" (Lam. 2:9, NASB). There was no prophetic word from God as instruction and encouragement for the people. They were left to try to see the meaning of their plight on their own. This concept of a vision from God is vital to our understanding of motivation for evangelism. In a sense we mean the same thing by *vision* that Jeremiah meant. We mean a clear word from God, an interpretation of the present state of affairs from the viewpoint of God and his purpose. It is true today as of old that "where there is no vision, the people are unrestrained, but happy is he who keeps the law" (Prov. 29:18, NASB).

One of the greatest challenges of Christian leadership today is to keep before the people a vision of God's purpose. Only then are they going to see their situation and their calling clearly. As we have said, it is easy to get "fogged in" to a merely human view of our evangelistic task. Then it becomes an almost unbearable weight. We must see the hand of God at work according to his announced purpose. We must be able to interpret our times and our task in light of what he is doing. It is only as our preachers declare the Word of God to us that we "see" as we should. Only with that vision from God through his Word does the seemingly impossible task of reaching our world become possible.

When Jesus saw the multitudes he was moved with compassion. He turned to his disciples and said, "The harvest is plentiful but the workers are few. Ask the Lord of the harvest, therefore, to send out workers into his harvest field" (Matt. 9:37-38). Jesus was realistic about the need for workers. But notice that he saw the multitudes as a harvest. From God's viewpoint, they were ready for the reaping. We see them so often as hard, cold, obstinate "stumps" to be dug up with greatest effort. God sees a harvest. Jesus urged them to ask the Lord of the harvest for workers for *his* harvest. Whose harvest is it? It is *his* harvest! We are but workers. God has taken upon himself the initiative, resources, power, and responsibility for the harvest.

There is probably no motivation stronger than an assurance of victory. Winners just run faster than losers. When we sense victory we tend to press on for the finish with greater zeal. As we keep before our people the biblical picture of a sovereign God who will ultimately accomplish his purpose, we place a vision of victory in their minds. Without this vision, the people languish away in pessimism and apathy. But seeing their place in the divinely assured scheme of redemption motivates them to action. The reverse side of this vision is the burden of the Lord, that compelling obsession which caused Paul to cry out, "I am compelled to preach. Woe to me if I do not preach the gospel!" (1 Cor. 9:16).

How do we get the people of God out of God's house and into God's world with the gospel! I am sure we have not given all the answers. Nevertheless, our sketch of these approaches to motivation may help clarify the dynamics involved in "getting out of the bunkhouse." There is no place here for manipulation, authoritarianism, or hypocrisy. Through all of these approaches to motivation runs the necessity of a sincere desire on the part of a leader to help fellow believers to be successful in their Christian service.

I have been impressed with how small the world becomes to a person who begins to lose his health. In a sickroom a person struggles to have a good day, to be free from pain for a few hours, to survive another day until time to sleep the fitful and restless sleep that illness allows. In an existence when health begins to diminish and a person spends all of his energies and attention staying alive one more day, the world becomes a small place indeed. The patient's world is within the four walls of his room or perhaps even this side of the curtain that separates him from his roommate.

His concern is for the intravenous feedings that sustain his life, for the hypodermic shots that keep him free from pain, for the simple comforts of a clean bed and a bath and a little kindness from family or friends. A big event may be the delivery of some flowers for the room or a day relatively free from pain. It is an exciting adventure when he can get to his feet and feebly walk out the door into the hallway. Life becomes small indeed. The world closes in to the space of but a few feet in either direction. How fortunate we are when we are healthy and able to live without having to spend all our energy just staying alive.

What a tragedy it is for a congregation to become that ill spiritually. What a tragedy when it begins to spend all of its energies just staying alive. What a tragedy when its world narrows to the limited space within the church building. What a tragedy when the primary effort of the church is to maintain peace and harmony among the members and to see that the financial statement stays in the black. What a tragedy when the outreach efforts of the church are primarily designed to enlist newcomers in the community who can strengthen the congregation in some way. What a tragedy when the church of Jesus Christ against which the gates of hell shall not be able to prevail is weak and debilitated like a tottering, desperately ill person.

Motivating persons is a challenge for those of us who seek to lead God's people. We need to awaken them to the reality of an almighty

God who is alive and well and to motivate Christian people to look beyond the limited vision of doing church work. It can be done. Church members can catch a vision of the church as the dynamic living body of Christ penetrating the entire community as salt and light. But we who would lead must motivate them for that work in every way we can.

10
Disciplined to Win

In the tropical forests of South and Central America lives the sloth, a fascinating animal about the size of a large cat. This slow-moving mammal gets his name from the fact that he usually appears lazy and sluggish. The toothless sloths live in trees, feeding on leaves and tender shoots, and hardly ever descend to the ground. In fact they move with great difficulty on the ground because their feet, equipped with long, hooklike toes, are adapted to their habit of hanging upside down from the limbs of trees. There are two varieties of these small animals, the three-toed sloth (Bradypus tridactylus) and the two- toed sloth (Choloepus hoffmanni), so named because of the number of claws on each front foot.

Another interesting variety of sloth is the five-toed sloth (Homo sapiens) which inhabits most areas of the civilized world. He is also known to be sluggish and lazy. He is toothless, thus having no bite, and spends most of his time up a tree. From his habit of hanging around out on a limb he gets a peculiar upside-down view of the world. He hardly ever gets down to earth and moves with great difficulty there when forced to do so. The mortal enemies of the five-toed sloth are responsibility and self-discipline.

This interesting animal is often mentioned in the ancient literature of the Hebrews, where he is called a "sluggard" and looked upon with distain. The five-toed sloth is often found under the circumstances. In fact, under almost any pile of circumstances you are likely to find one of these timid creatures. The cry of the five-toed sloth is a miserable whine which sounds something like "I couldn't help it," or "Why did this have to happen to me?"

Unfortunately, we all suffer from a likeness to the five-toed sloth. It is characteristic of human nature to avoid responsibility, get a cock-eyed view of life, make excuses for why we are irresponsible, and see ourselves at the mercy of the "circumstances." The sooner we can admit our humanity at this point and laugh at ourselves, the sooner we can take the challenge of personal responsibility and discipline seriously. The demands of real leadership cannot be met with irresponsibility, a distorted outlook, excuses, and self-pity. Leaders may well deserve the general-on-the-white-horse image they sometimes try to present. But somehow we are never far from our alter ego, the five-toed sloth.

Laodicean Leadership

It seems we are ever in a crisis of leadership in one sector or another. In the mid-seventies a rash of rather abrupt leadership changes saw Japan, Germany, the United States, Great Britain, and France all adjusting to new voices at the top. The perennial call for new political leadership in this country goes deeper in these days than mere election-year rhetoric. There seems to be a general lack of confidence in political leadership at any level. Anytime people suffer from poor leadership there is confusion, disharmony, uncertainty, a loss of creativity, a lessening of productive efficiency, a lack of purpose, enthusiasm, optimism, and hope.

Not only is this lack of confidence in leadership a fact in the political arena but in the church as well, and in many local congregations. Where are the great leaders today? Perhaps you could name a few. But closer to home, where are the local leaders who show the marks of greatness? I believe there is a leadership crisis in the churches today that may well prove more serious in the long run than the crisis of political leadership. Only when pastors and lay leaders earn the confidence of the people can the churches avoid the conditions described in Judges 21:25, "In those days there was no king in Israel; everyone did what was right in his own eyes."

If our churches are to meet the challenge of getting the good news to a tangled world, we must have effective leadership. The people will reflect those who lead them. If the leader has a sense of purpose and vision of what God is doing, the people will have a sense of purpose as well. If the leader is earnest and disciplined to the point of sacrifice, the people will tend toward a greater commitment and discipline. If the leader is confident of God's resources and sure of victory by his grace, the people will come to see themselves in more positive terms and expect success. If the leader has a servant's spirit and is generous, helpful, and compassionate, the people will become more sensitive to the needs of others and generous in their responses to them.

We are talking here about the man and who he is—not only about what he preaches or teaches or the stance he takes in public. It may well be that the true quality of one's character shows up best when he thinks no one is looking. No matter how gracious, courteous, affable, and witty a leader is in public, the true nature of the man will ultimately determine the quality of his leadership. This is true in politics and business to a large degree, but it is critical in Christian leadership. At the root of Christian character is a demand for consistency, genuineness, moral integrity, truthfulness, and confidence in God. A Christian leader who appears to have all the "right" qualities but doesn't ring true in his private life will leave discerning believers skeptical, uncertain, and disheartened.

Perhaps the greatest problem with our leaders is that so many do not appear to be aflame with a vision for God and his purpose. But neither are many of them so totally irresponsible that the churches feel justified in "throwing the bums out." Some of our pastors, deacons, and other leaders would admit that they are not flaming zealots. They don't want to be fanatical. But neither are they totally indifferent to the cause of Christ. They are not hot. But neither are they cold. Let's say they are moderate or just warm. Warm. That's it. They are lukewarm. "I know your deeds," said Jesus, "that you are neither cold nor hot. I wish you were either one or the other! So because you are lukewarm—neither hot nor cold—I am about to spit you out of my mouth" (Rev. 3:15-16).

The trouble with such "Laodicean leadership" is that their tepid example affects the congregation about the same way a warm bath affects me. It makes me drowsy, comfortable, and ready for "the land of nod"—which is where too many of our people are. Throughout history the really great leaders have been men of vision who knew where they were going and dared to challenge the people to sacrifice in getting there. It is not so much men of great natural gifts and cleverness who are needed as we face the challenge of world evangelization; it is rather men of vision, bold men who have been with God, men willing to accept the disciplines necessary to true Christian leadership.

A Vision Through the Fog

As we have said, it is easy to get fogged in in our outlook. We begin to see things from the viewpoint of human aims, human resources, and human talents. We lose sight of the great sweep of God's redemptive purpose. We lose sight of where we came from, why we are here, and where we are going. It seems that there is lacking among many pastors and lay leaders alike a clear-cut vision of spiritual realities of God and his purpose for the world. It is true that "where there is no vision the people perish" (Prov. 29:18, KJV). But it is also true that "the people who know their God will display strength and take action" (Dan. 11:32, NASB). One of the greatest needs we face is to recognize that since evangelism is a supernatural, God-initiated, eternally significant task, it must begin with a clear vision of God and his purpose.

What a source of strength it is to know that our sovereign heavenly Father fully intends to accomplish his purpose on this earth. "My purpose will be established," he said, " and I will accomplish all My good pleasure" (Isa. 46:10, NASB). This purpose of God was for Jesus the driving force that compelled him at every point to insist on the will of God. It was as though doing the will of God were his magnificent obsession. It was his "food" (John 4:34). It was the qualifying mark of his true kinsmen (Matt. 12:50). It was his mission in life (John 6:38). It was the mark of those who enter into the kingdom (Matt. 7:21). It was his prayer in the hour of greatest personal struggle (Luke 22:42).

A vision for God and his purpose comes only with the kind of confidence in him which affirms joyously and triumphantly that he "is able to do immeasurably more than all we ask or imagine, according to his power that is at work within us" (Eph. 3:20). We must accept his assurance that "we are more than conquerors through him who loved us" (Rom. 8:37) because he "always leads us in triumphal procession in Christ and through us spreads everywhere the fragrance of the knowledge of him" (2 Cor. 2:14). So we declare his Word with confidence because he has said, "It shall not return to Me empty, without accomplishing what I desire, and without succeeding in the matter for which I sent it" (Isa. 55:11, NASB).

Scripture narratives from the lives of many men indicate clearly that it is a vision of God and his purpose which kindles the smoldering zeal of his servants. Until Isaiah "saw the Lord sitting on a throne, lofty and exalted" he never bothered to say, "Here am I. Send me!" (Isa. 6:1, 8, NASB). Until David, on his face before the Lord, prayed, "Restore to me the joy of Thy Salvation," he was in no position to affirm, "Then I will teach transgressors Thy ways, and sinners will be converted to Thee" (Ps. 51:12-13, NASB). Evangelism is at the very heart of the purpose of God. When men open their own hearts to a vision of God and that purpose, they see as never before the challenge and promise of the evangelistic task.

With such a vision of God comes boldness for his purpose. After the visionary experience of Pentecost, the formerly cowering disciples of Jesus were new men in their boldness with the gospel. When they were commanded to cease preaching in the name of Jesus, they gathered for prayer. They did not ask for victory over their enemies, nor for success for the gospel in its proclamation, nor for safety from persecution, nor for comfort in their troubles. They asked for the one thing they needed most. They began their prayer, "Sovereign Lord, you made the heaven and the earth and the sea, and everything in them" (Acts 4:24), and then continued to exalt God and to rekindle their vision of his sovereig power.

Then their one rquest came: "Now, Lord, consider their threats and enable your servants to speak your word with great boldness. Stretch out your hand to heal and perform miraculous signs and wonders through the name of your holy servant Jesus" (Acts 4:29-30). At the close of that prayer the place was shaken, and those present were filled with the Holy Spirit and spoke the word of God boldly. Their prayer was for boldness, the boldness that comes from knowing that God is a God who can stretch out his hand to heal and perform miraculous signs and wonders through the name of Jesus.

Paul wrote from prison asking the believers to pray for him that he might fearlessly declare the gospel as he should (Eph. 6:19-20). He wrote urging Timothy to "fan into flame the gift of God" because "God did not give us a spirit of timidity, but a spirit of power, of love and of self-discipline. So do not be ashamed to testify about our Lord"

(2 Tim. 1:6-8). It seems clear that flagging evangelistic zeal and effectiveness come because of a loss of that spirit of boldness. That boldness is lost when Christians lose their vision of the sovereign God and his redemptive purpose. That vision is obscured when the fog of worldly concerns narrows our visibility to the circumstances and possibilities on a merely human level. That fog floats in when we fail to maintain the disciplines necessary to real discipleship.

The Dynamic of Personal Discipline

The one factor that may determine more than any other the effectiveness of a leader of God's people is personal discipline. There is a dynamic about discipline. It gives power to a person's life. Whether he is a musician, an athlete, or a Christian leader, the key to going beyond the ordinary is discipline. In any field notice the disciplined person. He is the one who feels good about what he's doing, is prepared for action, has put in all those hours doing what he may not have wanted to do but knew was necessary. As you look at our church leadership, do you see discipline like that? How many disciplined people do you know?

There is a direct correlation between personal Christian discipline and the spiritual boldness which is necessary to evangelistic zeal and effective leadership. When a person is disciplined in the areas appropriate to Christian discipleship he has a sense of preparedness, a sensitivity to God, a confidence in divine resources, and a courage in the cause of Christ. As a disciple walks close to his Lord in the Christian life, he has a vision of God's power and purpose. As a Christian leader he comes before the people as one who has been with God. He leads with a positive assurance of power and direction. His spirit is contagious. Those who work with him become more positive, more bold, more confident in God.

We know that those expressions of discipleship which are so necessary to Christian strength and growth are not natural to human nature. Real prayer is not a normal desire of the natural man. Neither is a serious study of the Scriptures. Nor is man normally going to "walk in the Spirit" or "wait on the Lord" as we are admonished to do. Yet anyone who would be strong in the Lord must be a man of prayer, Bible study, and a godly walk. The answer is discipline. Anyone who only prays when he feels like it will be a poor intercessor. Neither can we wait for inspiration before we study the Scripture and hide it in our hearts. So is walking "in the Spirit" (Gal. 5:16, NASB) a deliberate decision that calls for discipline. In fact, the whole of discipleship is a matter of self-denial and a determined loyalty to Christ—a question of discipline.

We are not talking here about some kind of good works which earns our salvation. We are saying that just as God gives a man the final choice in conversion, so he leaves him the choice in his Christian walk. Any of us can coast along without deliberately seeking to be strong in spirit or grow in Christ. But Christian growth requires taking the situation in hand and bringing our own lives under the rule of Christ. We are the stewards, the managers of our time, our energies, our gifts. It is up to each of us to take definite action in planning to develop spiritual strength by God's grace. The person who takes charge of his own personal growth in Christ will find his entire life situation responding to his control. He is not the five-toed sloth—ever under the circumstances. He is, rather, one who seeks to take charge of his situation under the lordship of Christ.

With our acknowledgment through personal discipline of the lordship of Christ, we experience a release of the power of God in and through our lives for moral and spiritual effectiveness. Actually, our discipline in the areas we have mentioned is an expression of our faith in God at those points. As we express faith God releases his grace; he always honors faith. So a disciplined Christian leader becomes bold, sees God work in his life in power, and becomes a representative of the very authority of God in his leadership.

Now that we have examined the effects of discipline in the life of Christian leaders, let's think with Paul about the necessity of Christian discipline. In his well-known discussion in 1 Corinthians 9 Paul gave several significant insights into the urgent need for discipleship in the lives of God's people. These truths are particularly relevant to the responsibility of church leadership.

Planning to Win

Discipline is necessary in the Christian life because that life is a winning life. Paul writes that in a race all run, but only one receives the prize. So he urged us to run in such a way as to win. He then emphasized that the one pressing to win will be disciplined in every respect (1 Cor. 9:24-25). It is a basic New Testament truth that we as believers are involved in the outworking of a victory. Paul wrote that "we are more than conquerors through him who loved us" (Rom. 8:37). God always causes us to triumph in every place (2 Cor. 2:14). Being certain of this victory is a great source of motivation for the Christian leader. Winners who know they are winners run like winners. They also act like winners at the point of training, making whatever preparation and discipline is necessary to one who is planning to win.

We have heard the axiom "It's not whether you win or lose, but how you play the game." But Paul seemed to be of a different mind when he wrote: "I press on toward the goal to win the prize for which God has called me heavenward in Christ Jesus" (Phil. 3:14). It may be true that many of the activities of life are of such a trivial nature that success is of no importance. In recreation and play, winning or losing is not nearly so important to the believer as maintaining a right Christian spirit. Some Christians seem to approach their commitment to Christ in the same indifferent way. But under the sovereignty of God the believer can know that no turn of circumstance is a win or a loss. He is not keyed to circumstances but to the purpose of God. So even though he does not judge his situation by any particular set of circumstances, he is nonetheless expectant of the kind of divinely graced life of effectiveness described in the New Testament.

This self-identity of the believer as a winner is rooted in the focus of his selfhood in Christ. It is derived from the nature of God as sovereign and all-powerful Creator. Unfortunately, some Christians, even leaders, do not think of themselves as winners. Their concept of self is attached to natural gifts and the unconsciously developed self-esteem that has taken shape even from childhood. These misinformed believers do not plan on winning. But there are so many questions we must ask of them. If you don't plan on winning, why are you in the race? Just jogging along for the fellowship? If you are not planning on winning, what are you planning to do? Lose? Then if you plan to lose and are programmed for it, there's no way you can win. It is a matter of faith—either faith in God's purpose or faith in a preconceived expectation of defeat. Let us believe God!

We must insist that the Christian life is a winning life. God is not dead! He has not changed his mind about his intention to complete fully his plans for the world. Rather than presuming upon this victory and apathetically riding its coattails, the believer who sees the biblical conception of the victory of Christ will be compelled to the kind of discipline which made that victory possible. He will want to "throw off everything that hinders and the sin that so easily entangles" because it was Jesus who, seeing the joyous victory set before him, endured even the shameful cross and "sat down at the right hand of the throne of God" (Heb. 12:1-2). So we praise God that we do not press toward a victory that awaits our strength; rather, we advance from a victory already complete in Christ. An inseparable element of involvement in that victory is the discipline characteristic of a true disciple of Jesus Christ.

Disciplined in All Things

Discipline is also necessary for the Christian because every aspect of life affects our fruitfulness and effectiveness in fulfilling God's will. Meeting the challenge of a tangled world with the gospel calls for a consistency touching every activity and interest of the believer. We cannot divide life into the religious and the secular or the spiritual and the physical. There is no area of our lives which is to be optional to the lordship of Christ. Paul wrote that those who strive to win are disciplined in "all things" (1 Cor. 9:25, NASB). Imagine a career athlete whose attitude is this: "It doesn't matter whether I make these training sessions. I'll perform on the field. It doesn't matter how I live on my own time. It doesn't matter about my eating, rest, or personal habits. I'll perform acceptably when it comes time for the game." There have been some like that, but they usually don't last.

What about the Christian who says it doesn't matter about the little things in his life? "It doesn't matter about my language. I'm still going to be spiritual enough. It doesn't matter about my family relationships. I know things are not good at home, but that's normal, isn't it? It doesn't matter. We're all human, aren't we? What do my personal habits have to do with my Christian service? Whose business is it how I handle my private affairs? I'll do my part when it comes to serving God. At least I'm not a hypocrite [as though there were some virtue in honest worldliness]. I know I've got my little inconsistencies, but they don't affect my church work." There are Christians who think like this, even among those we look to for leadership.

Is discipleship a part-time job? I can imagine interviewing Simon Peter about his life-style. "What is your occupation?" *I'm a disciple of Jesus of Nazareth.* "But I mean, What do you do for a living?" *Oh, I used to fish. That's my trade.* "What do you do in your spare time?" *What spare time?* We could also interview Paul. Here is a man who made his living as a tentmaker, but his occupation was "apostle to the Gentiles." No matter what he did, he never suspended his role as a disciple of Jesus Christ. No facet of his life was untouched by that commitment. He wrote of the discipline of body (1 Cor. 9:27), mind (Phil. 2:5), thoughts (2 Cor. 10:5), speech (Col. 4:6), actions (Rom. 13:13), and even eating and drinking (Rom. 14:21). Every facet of life and living was to be disciplined so that the Christian may "do it all for the glory of God" (1 Cor. 10:31).

A pastor friend recently talked with me about his battle with the problem of being overweight. He told me how many pounds he had taken off in the past few weeks by pushing away from the table and watching between-meal snacks—a matter of discipline. But he also told me that it seemed he was thinking clearer, was able to study better, and was able to be more consistent in his spiritual life. He said that from his own experience, he had determined that it is impossible to be spiritually disciplined if we are not physically disciplined. This seems to me to be consistent with the biblical emphasis on the unity of man.

Paul wrote, "I beat my body and make it my slave" (1 Cor. 9:27). He also wrote urging the believers at Rome to offer their bodies as living sacrifices. This most comprehensive term (bodies) in Paul's psychology means the whole man, with an emphasis upon the outward and active dimension. The Hebrew idea of body encompassed all that we are. If we cannot discipline our bodily activity, we should not expect much success in our discipline in purely spiritual matters. The Scripture indicates that we become the slaves of whatever master we submit to (Rom. 6:16). If you and I do not exercise our God-given control so that we can take all that we are and submit it to the will of God, then we are fooling ourselves to think we are going to have a spiritual dynamic about our lives.

A friend once shared with me sadly that his wife spent much of her time reading cheap mystery novels. She seemed obsessed with this useless pastime. As a result she had no interest in Bible study, prayer, or spiritual growth. The results in her own life were obvious. Though she was regularly involved in church activities they seemed to have little effect, if any, on the way she spent her time. So there are any number of diversions that take our time, energy, effort, and our resources. TV is a thief we pay to sit in our own homes and then rob us of hours of precious time. Some television programming may be useful to Christian nurture, ministry, or an understanding of our tangled world. But many Christians never turn their TV off and so spend hours wandering in the vast wasteland of TV viewing.

Every aspect of our everyday living affects our effectiveness as servants of God. Again, we must emphasize that the drive for personal discipline for a Christian is not the desire to earn his salvation or the fear he will lose it. We rather take in hand to "subdue the earth," beginning with our own lives, because we have been set free to exercise a godly control under the lordship of Christ. We seek ever to expand that territory of our own lives that is under the lordship of Christ. We hope to be the same kind of Christian when no one is looking as we are in public because every aspect of life is relevant to our discipleship.

Eternal Consequences

Important among reasons why discipline is necessary to the Christian is the fact that the consequences are eternal. Paul wrote that those athletes who strive to win the race do so "to get a crown of laurel that will not last; but we do it to get a crown that will last forever" (1 Cor. 9:25). He told the believers at Thessalonica that they were themselves his hope, his joy, and his crown (1 Thess. 2:19). Though the victory is already won in the atonement of Christ, the results for mankind are yet dependent upon the dedication, discipline, and divinely graced service of believers everywhere. What we do or fail to do definitely affects the redemptive program of God. How we are disciplined for the race affects our effectiveness.

Paul wrote toward the close of his own ministry, "I have fought the good fight, I have finished the race, I have kept the faith. Now there is in store for me the crown of righteousness, which the Lord, the righteous Judge, will award to me on that day" (2 Tim. 4:7-8). The Christian's faithfulness throughout his ministry determines the nature of his reward in heaven. The sort of life and ministry one builds upon his foundation in Christ will be tested in "that Day," and the believer either will receive a reward or suffer loss on the basis of the quality of his work (1 Cor. 3:11-15).

Due to their great interest in sports, my boys and I have discussed several times the matter of professional athletics. We have noted that professional athletes usually have a short period of time in which to make their mark. A man approaching forty is often considered old. Recently a baseball star whose career reached its height during my teen years appeared on television doing a commercial. Of course, the boys didn't know who he was. Names are on the lips of millions one year and forgotten the next. All of the training, the discipline, the sacrifice are for a moment's glory. But the Christian crown is incorruptible. It relates to the lives of those he has served in the name of Christ. It relates to his faithfulness. It is good forever.

Jesus told the parables of the tower builder and the king going to war in order to talk about preparedness and adequacy for the task. A builder will make sure he has enough materials and a king enough warriors. We usually interpret his "count the cost" statement to mean that we are to count the cost. But we have nothing to lose and everything to gain. No, Jesus is counting the cost because he is a King at war and the Builder of a kingdom. If every disciple were of the quality that you and I are, what sort of material would Jesus be working with? Think of the people around us whose lives could be changed by the dynamic power of God that comes in a disciplined Christian life. The stakes are high. The cost is great.

The Measure of Commitment

Discipline in the Christian life is the one thing that best indicates the degree of a person's earnest, sacrificial commitment to Christ. A believer can get very emotional about his relationship with Jesus. He can enjoy church. He can love the hymns and the sermons. He can have wonderful, nostalgic memories of the things that have happened in the church in the past. He can get excited and really enjoy an opportunity to sing, teach, or preach. He can be as regular as Sunday in his attendance at church meetings. A Christian can use a liberal sprinkling of "hallelujahs" and "praise the Lords" as he talks. He can even develop a serious and particularly sanctified expression on his face. He can put Christian bumper stickers on his car. He can have wonderful spiritual experiences. There can be a number of different distinctions about any of us, but the one that best indicates whether we mean business about following Jesus Christ is discipline.

There is ample admonition in the Scriptures urging us to be holy because God is holy (Lev. 19:2; 2 Cor. 7:1; Heb. 12:14; 1 Pet. 1:15-16). But holiness is not an emotion or an affectation. We are not charged to *appear* holy but to *be* holy and to behave accordingly. This holiness is a Christian distinctiveness, an uncommonness of thought, word, and deed that marks us as followers of Christ. The nature of this holiness is well defined in the Scriptures in terms of rejecting that which is of the "flesh" and the "world" and embracing a new moral life in Christ. There is no way that the outworking of this holiness comes in the believer's life apart from personal discipline. Any command implies choice. Any continual choice calls for discipline. Any discipline reveals the level of one's determination and commitment.

We are given other charges in the Scriptures that call for discipline. A Christian does not merely fall into an effective and consistent discipleship. It is no accident when a believer's life is marked by growth in Christ, increasing insight into the Scriptures, a greater sensitivity to to the needs of others, a growing evangelistic concern, a distinctive moral responsibility. We are admonished to walk in the Spirit, but this is a daily choice and discipline (Gal. 5:16). We are urged to wait on the Lord, but this is not normal to the natural man and requires a disciplined confidence in the providence of God (Ps. 27:14). We are given many references as to the value of the Scriptures in the life of of a believer, but study and memorization are matters of discipline.

You may be thinking that this sounds like a form of legalism. But I must insist that I am here describing the discipline and consistency necessary for spiritual survival in a tangled world. We do not think it a dead keeping of the law when an athlete follows a rigorous training schedule. He has a goal. His imagination burns with a dream. So has the Christain been set aflame with a desire to honor God, to live only for the One who has saved him. There is no place in Christianity for works religion, which tries to earn God's acceptance. We do not seek to discipline ourselves to improve our position with God so that he will love us more or accept us better. That's all settled in Christ. I can never be more acceptable or more loved than I am now.

We press for personal discipline because it is a part of the plan of God for our lives. Paul wrote that "we are God's workmanship, created in Christ Jesus to do good works, which God prepared in advance for us to do" (Eph. 2:10). "I urge you," he wrote, "in view of God's mercy, to offer yourselves as living sacrifices, holy and pleasing to God" (Rom. 12:1). "Continue to work out your salvation with fear and trembling," he wrote, "for it is God who works in you to will and to act according to his good purpose" (Phil. 2:12-13). His own formula for this disciplined ministry was clear when he said, "To this end I labor, struggling with all the energy he so powerfully works in me" (Col. 1:29). We accept the discipline of a follower of Christ not as the burden of legalism, but with the assurance that God is at work. This discipline, more than any quality about us, will indicate the level of our dedication as disciples of Jesus Christ.

The Castaways

Discipline is necessary in the Christian life because those who are undisciplined will be set aside. Paul wrote, "I do not run like a man running aimlessly; I do not fight like a man shadow boxing. No, I beat my body and make it my slave so that after I have preached to others, I myself will not be disqualified for the prize" (1 Cor. 9: 26-27). He obviously was committed wholeheartedly to his calling in Christ. He was not playing. He meant business. No sacrifice was so great, no task so difficult, no obstacle so insurmountable that it could be allowed to stand in the way.

Some of us may not like the sound of the severity and seeming ruthlessness attributed to God in this passage. Would our loving heavenly Father be so harsh? Would he actually disqualify one of his choice servants? Is God that unsympathetic with the difficulty, even the impossibility, of the task to which he has called us? Does he not realize what a burden we bear and how often it seems we will be crushed under its weight? Yes, he knows. "For we do not have a high priest who is unable to sympathize with our weaknesses, but we have one who has been tempted in every way, just as we are—yet was without sin" (Heb. 4:15). Jesus was God himself, accepting the call of the cross. He knows what we face. "Consider him who endured such opposition from sinful men, so that you will not grow weary and lose heart" (Heb. 12:3).

The horror of the cross should show us the answer we seek in this apparent lack of sympathy on the part of God. God intends to see his purpose fulfilled in the redemption of man. He has determined that nothing will defeat that purpose. His plan is to use men to accomplish that purpose. Yet he has chosen to grant man the freedom to accept or reject his will. The fallen state of the world raises serious obstacles to God's program of redemption. Nevertheless, he will not be deterred. God is just that serious about completing his mission of grace and love. Neither Satan, nor sin, nor willful man, nor difficulties of any kind will cause him to change his plans.

In light of this irrevocable purpose of God, we can better understand Paul's determination. Will a God who so loves mankind that he would send his own Son to the cross for them take it lightly when his own servants are undisciplined and irresponsible? Does God have any choice then but to set them aside? Is it unreasonable to think that if you are not going to get into the race, you should get out of the way? But let us not develop a martyr complex about our impossible calling. God never calls anyone to a task except as he provides all the resources necessary for that task. It is not a question of power. Remember that he shall supply all our needs (Phil. 4:19) and that his grace is sufficient (2 Cor. 12:9). Ours is not to be able, but to be making those daily choices of faith that open our lives to the power of God as instruments of his purpose.

You have seen them as I have—the used-to-be's, the could-have-been, the dropouts, the castaways. Why is it that effective and promising Christian leaders are set aside? If we could take a poll, we might come up with interesting statistics. But we already know from observation some of the answers. The most blatant castaways are those who are publicly exposed as immoral, dishonest, or heretical. But a second problem group is the dropouts who were once faithful and apparently effective leaders. In most cases I believe these folk knew some time in advance that they had been set aside or wanted out. We must learn better how to minister to each of these groups. In our humanity none of us are immune to failure. We must help bear one another's burdens.

A third group of castaways is that large corps of Christians who are leaders in name only. These are the ones who have lost, or never had, the spiritual dynamic that comes in a disciplined life. They have a position of responsibility that should be filled by a disciplined and effective leader, but it is only that position which gives them some semblance of leadership. As we have said, discipline is an expression of faith. If you have no real confidence in God and his purpose, you will not likely pay the price of discipline to participate in the fulfillment of that purpose. A lack of confidence in God's Word issues in a lack of discipline in study and memorization. A lack of confidence in God's providence issues in a lack of discipline in waiting on the Lord.

We are not surprised that God uses men who trust him and are committed to his purpose, men who accept the discipline consistent with discipleship. Neither should we be surprised when God does not use men who fail to trust him, are not committed to his purpose, and will not accept the necessity of discipline. There are many other factors involved, of course, but God in his sovereignty will be true to his nature and purpose as he has made them known to us in the Scriptures. We can reject the biblical construction of reality in favor of a version more in keeping with our own life-style. But this does not change what God will do. His purpose will be accomplished. All along the path of that redemptive program will be empty reminders of what might have been.

One day God went down to a remote part of the desert to talk with a shepherd and ex-prince of Egypt called Moses. He said, "Moses, I have seen the affliction and oppression of my people in Egypt. I have heard their cry. I know their sorrows and I have come down to deliver them. Now, Moses, I will send you to lead them out of that bondage." Moses began to make excuses: "Who am I to do this? They won't believe me. I'm not a good talker" (see Ex. 3:7-11). At every point the sovereign God of the universe patiently answered these objections with a promise of his grace. Then we can imagine the multitudes of weary slaves in Egypt as they stop their toil for a brief moment. It is almost as though they are aware somehow of the conversation going on in that desert. A hush falls among the angels of heaven and the weary multitudes on earth as God waits for a man to make up his mind.

God has chosen to use men to carry out his great redemptive purpose. What an amazing and astonishing fact. Yet it is true. He awaits the response of committed, obedient, disciplined men. The whole of salvation is accomplished in a man, Jesus of Nazareth, the Christ. In a garden Jesus and a few of his closest followers pause for a moment. Then he leaves them to go a bit farther and fall to his knees in prayer. After a while he returns to find his weary companions asleep. He urges them to watch with him and pray. He cries out in agony as the cross casts its shadow of horror over him. He prays, "If it is possible, may this cup be taken from me" (Matt. 26:39). He pauses, and it seems that time stops with him. Again the angels of heaven and now the unborn multitudes of lost mankind down through the ages to come turn, silent and weary, to listen while Almighty God waits for a man to make up his mind. The word comes, firm and determined, knowing well the cost: "Not as I will, but as you will."

Today God comes to you saying, "I have seen the affliction and oppression of my people in sin. I have heard the silent cry of their groping hearts. I know their sorrows, and I have come down to deliver them. Now, I will send you to declare to them my salvation and offer them my invitation to believe." But what difference does it make. You are alone. No one knows. Yet we can imagine the unseen, unknown faces amid the crowds in a tangled world. They don't know why, but they stop for a moment as though waiting for something. With these for whom Christ died, the angels in heaven pause in silence while God waits for a mere man to make up his mind.